To Clive & Amanda
    for Christmas 2011
a signed copy for you to keep
& read when you go to Studland!

    love    & best wishes

Dad & Anne.

# The Book of
# STUDLAND

To John and Rosemary

RODNEY LEGG

with the author's warm regards,

on Studland beach

HALSGROVE

*Rodney Legg*

1st December 2002

First published in Great Britain in 2002

*This book is dedicated to Studland villagers and guardians Geoff and Greta Hann.*

Frontispiece photograph: *Shell Bay and the harbour entrance in a view by Edwin Dodshon, north to Sandbanks and the Haven Hotel in 1927. The notice in the foreground warns about sailing risks in Studland Bay.*

**British Library Cataloguing-in-Publication Data**
A CIP record for this title is available from the British Library

ISBN 1 84114 149 6

**HALSGROVE**

Halsgrove House
Lower Moor Way
Tiverton, Devon EX16 6SS
Tel: 01884 243242
Fax: 01884 243325
email: sales@halsgrove.com
website: www.halsgrove.com

Printed and bound in Great Britain by Bookcraft Ltd., Midsomer Norton

*Whilst every care has been taken to ensure the accuracy of the information contained in this book, the publisher disclaims responsibility for any mistakes which may have been inadvertently included.*

# CONTENTS

*Introduction*      5

*Acknowledgements*      7

*Chapter 1:* STACKS, STONES & ROCKS      9

*Chapter 2:* HARBOUR, HEATH & HILLS      21

*Chapter 3:* PREHISTORIC & ROMAN TIMES      41

*Chapter 4:* CHURCH, CROSS & CASTLE      45

*Chapter 5:* NEWTON & GOATHORN      55

*Chapter 6:* PIRATES & PLUNDER      65

*Chapter 7:* PILOTS & FERRYMEN      69

*Chapter 8:* SHIPWRECKS & SALVAGE      75

*Chapter 9:* EMPIRE, SOLDIERS & WARS      81

*Chapter 10:* VILLAGE SCENES & PEOPLE      99

*Chapter 11:* NATURE & THE NATIONAL TRUST      145

*Subscribers*      157

*Suitably high-profile wind turbine beside the new Studland Study Centre next to Knoll Beach car park, photographed by Rodney Legg in 2000.*

# INTRODUCTION

For a boy from Bournemouth, Sandbanks was alluring, but Shell Bay and Studland were the ultimate seaside. Even from our home sands they were all part of the view with the chalk cliffs of Old Harry Rocks forming the backdrop. Discovery time unfolded as demilitarisation removed mines and other obstacles, as the last of the flying-boats lay at anchor in Poole Harbour, in a landscape that was in transition from war and austerity to peace and plenty. Excitement lurked in the dunes and the bushes with colourful lizards and snakes. Buses and bicycles made all this accessible to adventurous lads in an age when the young were allowed their freedom. Winton schoolmasters Victor Loosemore, Roy Parker and David Popham acquiesced, and not just in relatively safe territory such as Studland, letting me go off alone and climb Plynlimon to find the source of the River Severn.

From 1960 onwards this boyish enthusiasm for outdoor fun was accompanied by an obsessive desire to collect information. Even now I come across old blue notebooks which flop open with self-gathered material including the first interviews by one of life's born reporters. Langton Matravers headmaster Bernard Calkin cultivated my archaeological leanings and showed me where he had dug up Roman stone-cists in Studland churchyard. Much of the information derived from storytelling and a graphic account of Waterloo veteran William Lawrence, from the time when the Bankes Arms was the Duke of Wellington, came from David Popham's researches in the club-room library at Dorset County Museum. I remember enthusiastically staking out Hill Close on finding that Sir Herbert Cook had inherited from his grandfather, Sir Francis Cook, one of the best collections of Old Master paintings in England. I disappeared with embarrassment into the bushes on learning that he had died in 1939, and missed another trick by not asking *Titanic* survivor Jacob Gibbons to sign my six contemporary postcards featuring the world's most famous shipwreck.

*Edwardian Shell Bay and its ferry from Sandbanks* (right) *with Brownsea Island in the background* (left).

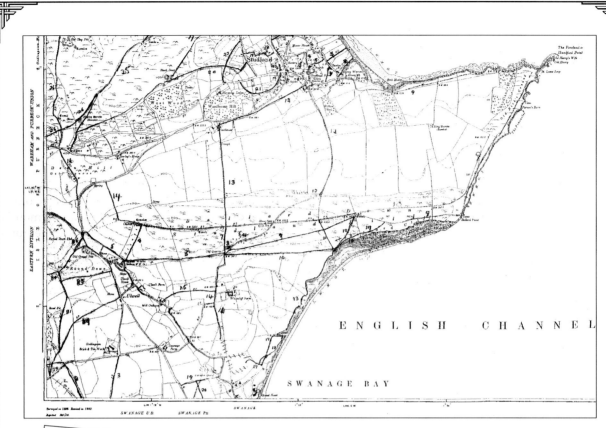

Above: *The village of Studland and its coastal downland.*

Left: *Composite post-war postcard view that sums up Studland's charms.*

Right: *More seaside views for arrivals on the ferry.*

# ACKNOWLEDGEMENTS

I do try and credit work when I know its source but it was only when researching Studland that I came across a mention of Bournemouth solicitor Edwin Dodshon and realised he was the landscape photographer from the 1920s whose pictures I bought at auction three decades ago. Before that I only knew his initials and had been told he was a pharmacist. His work was brought up to date half a century later by Colin Graham, until he left for Australia in 1985, who was one of the last in these parts to work in black and white and produce all his own prints.

The other timely discovery, in Waterstone's Bookshop at Bournemouth University, was Rosemary Chinchen. That name, for all its oriental sound, belongs to old Swanage and its stone mines. Jimmy Chinchen married Rosemary Payne, the daughter of Alec and Eileen Payne from Studland's principal family of fishermen and boatmen of Vine Cottage and Sea Coombe, in Beach Road. Great-grandfather Charlie Payne, who came from Lulworth Cove, started boating from Studland in 1885 after serving with the Royal Navy in Africa. Great-grandson Hugh Payne provided me with a superb archive showing the village at work and play.

Hardly any books have been consulted but informants have been legion. From meetings with Canon Douglas O'Hanlon in the 1970s, at the instigation of Hugh Sandall, to excursions with George Willey in the new millennium, I have been introduced to Studland villagers. These included Colonel Kenneth du Bois Ferguson, of the 77th Armoured Engineers, who as a young major laid steel-mesh mats across the sands in the D-Day landings. That technique had been perfected at Studland. After the war he bought Knoll House Hotel from Commander Chris Smith. Colonel Ferguson had his motorcycle blown up – as he went to mount it – and found a fellow traveller in Mrs May Morley Worton, who arrived in Studland by pony and trap in 1916 and progressed to her first Enfield in 1925. Within a year she could claim to have given a thrilling ride to almost all the younger villagers and had a 'guest book' listing some 150 of them. She died in 1990.

Much of the latter-day story has come from Rees Cox of the Nature Conservancy and Geoff Hann of the National Trust, plus briefings from property manager Julian Homer, and the encouragement of Celia Mead in the Wessex Regional Office. Some of the 'Cinderella' attractions of the Trust's vast expanse of newly accessible land now have a much higher profile thanks to their efforts. In preparing the material for this book I have been distracted by diversions on the ground, literally, to provide information and illustrations for panels describing Fort Henry and Fayle's Tramway. The other pleasure has been seeing the book into print, thanks to the patience of designer Katy Charge, who brought it all together.

*Edwardian view of Middle Beach,*
*north-westwards from Redend Point.*

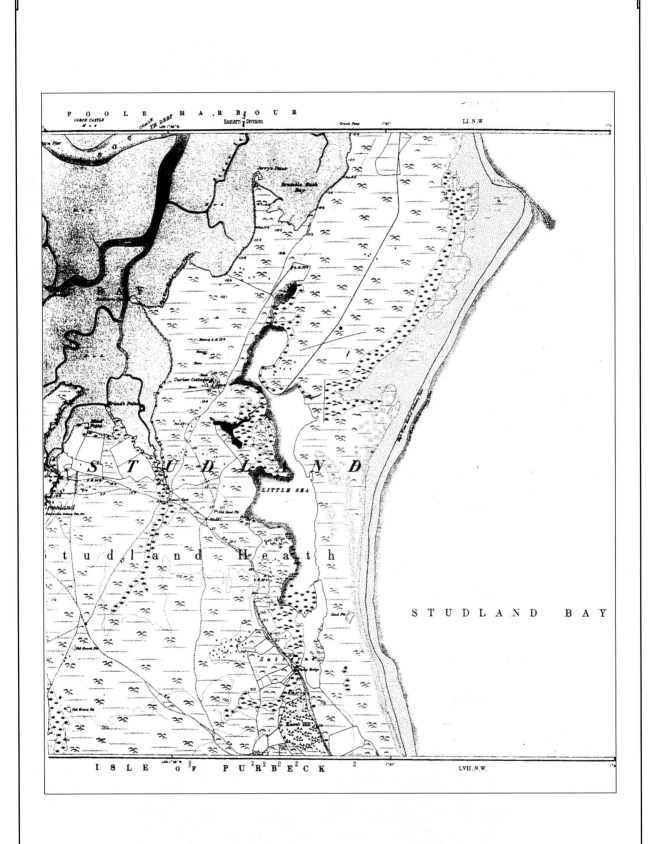

*Little Sea* (centre) *and Studland Bay in 1900.*

# Chapter 1

# STACKS, STONES & ROCKS

The Agglestone is the greatest of the natural boulders that are strewn across Godlingston Heath and adjacent Studland Heath. It dominates a knoll in the heather-clad National Nature Reserve between the Isle of Purbeck Golf Course and Studland village. The gritty golden blocks are iron-impregnated sandstone from a hard layer which formerly capped the sands and clays of the Bagshot beds, leaving remnants on steep-sided hillocks between shallow valleys filled with peat.

The public path from the golf links to Wadmore climbs the Agglestone knoll and passes the stone which is known in the village as the Rock. It is both an ancient and modern landmark in an otherwise featureless heath. All of this landscape, from the Purbeck Hills to the sea, is in the ownership of the National Trust which inherited the Corfe Castle Estate on the death of Ralph Bankes in 1981. That includes the golf course which Enid Blyton leased for her husband's amusement.

Being the biggest stone in the area, the Agglestone inspired a mass of folklore, and the name itself has roots in the supernatural. It probably means 'hagol-stone' – the Old English word for 'hailstone' – suggesting that it was thought to have fallen from the sky. Not that either name has much currency these days. 'Is this the way to the Rock?' a young couple asked me. It has a regular stream of admirers, including students of land-form geology, who carry out their main heathland studies in the dunes of Studland's famous nudist beach.

The advantage of visitor traffic is that the immediate vicinity is surrounded by soft white sand. Thousands of feet keep it well churned. Otherwise the Agglestone would be virtually engulfed in gorse scrub like the Puckstone which lies to the north-west. The latter takes its name from 'puca' – meaning 'goblin' – perhaps because it appears to come and go among the vegetation.

Charles Warne, Dorset's nineteenth-century antiquary, recorded the folklore and kept an open mind on the Agglestone:

*The anvil-shaped Agglestone, sketched from the south-west by Julia M. Colson, in the 1850s.*

# The Agglestone

*The Agglestone as it used to look, in a view north-eastwards towards Shell Bay and Bournemouth, in 1960.*

Right: *The path up the Agglestone knoll looked much the same in 1973, photographed by Frederick G. Masters, but 'the Rock' had fallen on its side.*

*The Agglestone, with the author on top for scale, pictured from the south-west by John Pitfield in 1981.*

# The Agglestone

Above: *The former flat top of the Agglestone tilting towards the surrounding sand, in a moody shot from the south, by Colin Graham in 1985.*

Below: *The Puckstone, photographed from the south-east by Colin Graham in 1985, in a view across Godlingston Heath to the conifers of the Rempstone Estate.*

*The country people say of it that his Satanic majesty (who is often a very important personage in these capricious parts) was one day sitting on the Needles Rock, Isle of Wight, whence, espying Corfe Castle in the distance, he took the cap from his head and threw it across the sea, with the intent of demolishing that structure. But it would appear that he over-estimated his powers of jactation, for the missile fell short of its mark, and there it stands to this day on Studland Heath, a monument of disappointed malice, a wonder to the peasantry, and a theme of antiquarian conjecture.*

This speculation might have ended long ago, when geologists explained that the Agglestone was in no way mysterious and had not been taken to Studland Heath by a glacier, the devil, prehistoric man, or anything else. It does, however, retain some residual interest for archaeologists, in that Bronze-Age man had dragged the boulders of the Rempstone stone circle, below the Purbeck Hills, from hereabouts. The Agglestone is to Rempstone what Preseli Mountain and Fyfield Down are to Stonehenge. Megalithic stones came from sacred places.

In 2000 I came across a couple of New Age travellers with hazel diviners, who were challenging the tangled terrain and trying to establish that a ley-line linked the Agglestone and Rempstone, towards Corfe Castle. Having explained to me the significance of the shape and alignment of the Rock, which they had watched me climb, they asked if I could also

'feel the energy'. They were somewhat miffed when I explained that I remembered it standing and looking quite different. It was a great anvil-shaped stone, about 16 feet high and twice that width across the top, weighing an estimated 400 tons. It became a natural wonder of eastern Purbeck because of its almost mushroom-like profile and the bonus of a glorious position offering fabulous views of Studland Bay and Poole Harbour.

The panorama remains but the stone itself took a tumble in September 1970 and collapsed on its side. The top, with a patina of centuries of undisturbed grey lichens, now slopes to the south, with a few sprigs of heather clinging to the fissures. The underlying stone is wine-red, across the harder stratum, softening to browns and yellows below. 'Its colour is just like Ayers Rock,' an Australian backpacker observed, 'but that's a bit bigger.'

He added that the Aboriginal people hold Ayers Rock sacred, and ask visitors to desist from climbing it, in another side-swipe against finding me on top of the Agglestone. No one from Studland was there to say the same but this must be their oldest sacred place.

In the village associations are made between the Rock and witchcraft but this appears to derive from stories that originated around a century ago about an old lady who became a recluse and set up home in a shack on the heath near the Agglestone. She shared it with an enormous black cat and soon established a reputation as a witch, compounded by the fact that the cat was aggressive and could not be approached.

*Romantically stormy Edwardian watercolour of Old Harry Rocks produced as a postcard in 1902.*

# Old Harry

"The Stacks".

*Stacks and the beach in 1905.*

*Old Harry in 1890, with a boatman rowing out from an intact Old Harry's Wife*
(right), *seen from rock pools to the north-east.*

## *Old Harry*

Left: *Stacks and steamers in 1910.*

*Paddle-steamer heading southwards off Old Harry Rocks in 1905.*

# Old Harry

Left: *Old Harry Rocks, from seawards to the south-east, photographed in 1925 by William Powell.*

Right: *Aerial view of Old Harry Rocks in 1935, from the east, showing open downland across Old Nick's Ground.*

*Chalk arch under Old Harry Rocks, photographed by Frederick G. Masters in 1959.*

# Old Harry

Main picture: *Old Harry Rocks and Ballard Point, in a view south-westwards from above Studland Bay by Richard Riding in 1975. The photograph was taken ahead of National Trust ownership, which brought about the restoration of Old Nick's Ground on the cliff top to grassland.*

Inset: *The view south-westwards over Old Harry Rocks and Ballard Point in 1959, towards Swanage, shortly before the ploughing of the coastal chalklands.*

# Old Harry

*Old Harry Rocks, looking south-eastwards from Redend Point, pictured by Colin Graham in 1983.*

*Sky smudges of gulls in flight during a time exposure of Old Harry Rocks, looking north-eastwards towards Bournemouth, by Colin Graham in 1985.*

*Turf Rick Rock, from Parson's Barn Cave, engraved by Philip Brannon in the 1850s.*

It was believed by villagers to be her 'familiar spirit' and was given as the excuse that no one investigated when the old lady was no longer seen during a cold winter. She was found to have died in a state of abject neglect.

The devil by another name also makes an appearance around Studland's other gems of land-form geology. Old Harry Rocks are the creation of coastal erosion, which leaves blocks of chalk known as stacks standing independently of the parent cliff. The slender one at the end of the The Foreland, or Handfast Point, is Old Harry. He had a plump wife who drowned in the 1896 gale that destroyed the old chain pier at Brighton.

The cliff top beside the chalk stacks and stumps is known as Old Nick's Ground. The detached section of cliff between the coast path and Old Harry is called No Man's Land. The gap between it and the mainland is St Lucas Leap. Saint Lucas is said to have been a pedigree greyhound that didn't quite make the jump when coursing a hare. Chalk stacks to the south,

*The Haystack, previously known as Turf Rick Rock, viewed from the north-east by Colin Graham in 1985.*

towards Ballard Down, are Turf Rick Rock – which locals call the Haystack – and the Pinnacle. Beside them, behind a shingle beach, Parson's Barn is a huge sea cave, 100 feet deep, 90 feet high, and 50 feet wide. Its name is an allusion to the days of tithes when the ecclesiastical barns, as at Abbotsbury and Cerne Abbas, were the biggest in the land. Collectively the stacks are known as Old Harry Rocks (The Foreland and Handfast Point are only ever used by map makers).

The continuation of the Purbeck Hills, eastwards, is to the Needles. Whilst the rivers running out of Poole Harbour and from Christchurch headed eastwards through the Solent, and the sea had yet to break through and capture Poole Bay, you could still have walked across to the Isle of Wight. That was the situation until about 12,000BC, only a blink in geological time, after which sea levels rose by approximately 100 feet as the last Ice Age relented and polar glaciations released a significant quantity of the world's water.

## The Haystack

*Cormorants on the Haystack,*
*photographed by Colin Graham in 1985.*

# The Pinnacle

*A classic shot of the lesser chalk stacks, the Haystack and the Pinnacle, in a view south-westwards towards Swanage in 1930.*

*Looking down on the Pinnacle, from the cliff to the west, in 1985.*

# Chapter 2

# HARBOUR, HEATH & HILLS

*The 'Excise Boat' beached on the sand at Shell Bay for use as a Coastguard Station,
drawn by Alfred Dawson in 1882.*

Stretching inland, along the southern side of the parish, are the uplifted chalk formations of compacted calcium from creatures of the Cretaceous sea. Northwards the landscape may look and feel wild and ancient but it has a modern geological dynamic as a succession of Bournemouth beaches have been swept around Poole Bay and deposited on the heathland shore. As groynes, concrete promenades, and other sea defences along the hotel coast have reduced the supply, the situation has become unsustainable. The result, for the first time in living memory, has been a net erosion of Studland sand and a return of seaweed and other marine life not usually associated with the best beach in Britain.

Maps of the seventeenth century show the South Haven peninsula as a narrow northward spit to the ferry point opposite the North Haven at Sandbanks, which was still shown as 'The Sandbanks' on the 6-inch Ordnance Survey Map in 1890.

The North Haven remained the dry peninsula but the contrasting wet peninsula of the South Haven used to be a matching sandy spit. It was the subsequent accumulation of sand on the eastern side of the Ferry Road that captured the outlet from a marsh and created the freshwater landlocked lagoon known as Little Sea between 1700 and 1850. The sand was still accumulating on the beach at a fast rate until 1960, when I laid out recent editions of the 6-inch Ordnance Survey Map, calculating that the high-water mark was advancing seawards at 10 yards a year, for my first teenage essay on local geography.

Little Sea is one of the few natural lakes in southern England. As with the many and varied snakes and lizards that live in this area, its presence was integral to the Nature Conservancy Council's decision to choose Studland Heath as the site for the creation of a National Nature Reserve. There is

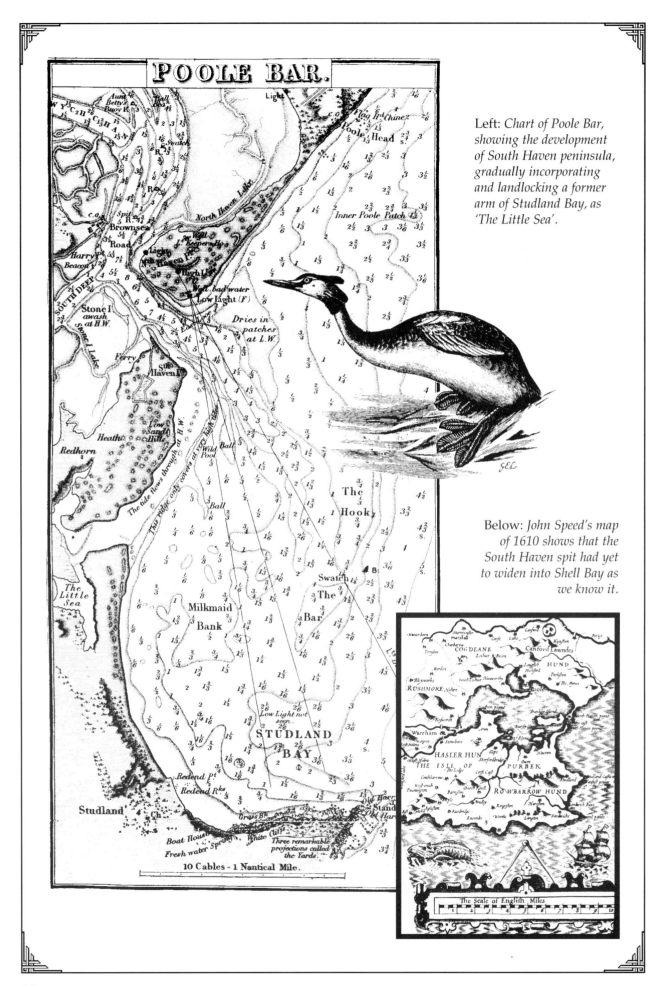

**POOLE BAR.**

*Left: Chart of Poole Bar,
showing the development
of South Haven peninsula,
gradually incorporating
and landlocking a former
arm of Studland Bay, as
'The Little Sea'.*

*Below: John Speed's map
of 1610 shows that the
South Haven spit had yet
to widen into Shell Bay as
we know it.*

10 Cables - 1 Nautical Mile.

# Shell Bay

*Shell Bay became the most famous beach in the area. The author's family from Bournemouth were there in 1928. His mother, Gladys Legg, is to the left of the case in the foreground, and father Ted Legg is on the right.*

**Inset:** *Shell Bay buildings* (right) *and pier* (centre left) *in a picture by Edwin Dodshon in 1927, looking north-eastwards towards the ferry kiosk and Haven Hotel* (centre) *on the Sandbanks side of the harbour entrance.*

**Main:** *Buildings at Shell Bay, one advertising a 'Disabled Ex-Serviceman', in a 1927 study by Edwin Dodshon looking south-east from the remains of the pier extending towards Stone Island and Branksea Castle.*

a guidebook fallacy about Little Sea – doubtfully ascribed to an old Studland legend – 'that it was into this that Sir Bedivere, that last of the Knights of the Round Table, cast King Arthur's great sword Excalibur, at the mortally-wounded Arthur's command' to be received by a mystic hand 'in whose keeping it remains until Arthur shall come again to rule.'

Unfortunately, no amount of suspended belief or folklore research can make that come true, given that Little Sea was formed in comparatively recent history. There is more truth, however, in the story of a murder that took place at South Haven Inn which, with nearby Gotchabed Cottages, collapsed into the expanding sand dunes before the First World War. 'Gotch-a-bed?' or a sound like it was the plea of stranded ferry passengers across the ages. Curlew Cottages, midway along the main spine of the peninsula, were demolished in 1925 to provide bricks as hardcore for the nearby Ferry Road. A drawing by Alfred Dawson, in 1882, does confirm the tale that a beached gunboat guarded the sands in about 1860. It was a newly-built warship, laid down during the Crimean War in 1854, which arrived too late to join the Baltic Fleet as the conflict against Russia drew to a close in 1856.

She was then seconded to Her Majesty's Customs and Excise, towards the end of the great smuggling era, and drawn up into the sands at the modern ferry point (SZ 037 867). Dawson's print shows Branksea Castle in the background, across the water to the north-west. The boat remained in use for about 15 years but the location was always unpopular, in splendid isolation on the 'wrong side' of the harbour, and the hulk was said to have become increasingly uncomfortable. The Coastguard Service then built permanent quarters on the Sandbanks peninsula, within walking distance of Poole, and the beached warship became redundant. She was still potentially seaworthy, as was proved by a Poole shipbuilder, who bought the vessel and refitted her as a three-masted schooner. There was also a cabin-like Coastguard Station on Studland Beach which remained in use until the Armistice in 1918. Alfred Newnham, the Chief Officer of the Coastguard Station, had five men working for him in 1890 and the same level of staffing applied under William Thorndale in 1915.

The dusky cockroach (*Ectobius lapponicus*) is found along these dunes, in the widest range of conditions from dry slopes to lush carrs, and David Ragge searched there for Cepero's ground-hopper (*Tetrix ceperoi*). He failed to find it but the lesser cockroach (*Ectobius panzeri*) was comparatively common. An intermediate zone of sallow and birch scrub has turned into oak woodland towards Knowle Hill (its original spelling) and Knoll Beach. Further on from the dense undergrowth east of Little Sea there is a belt of gorse bushes followed by sandy ridges, where former sand dunes are succumbing to a carpet of vegetation. Towards the real sea, the outer dunes have circular blow-outs where swirling particles in the air have resisted compaction and

*Tables and chairs to a background of cards and boxes of McVitie and Price's biscuits in Bakers Cabin at Shell Bay in 1928.*

*Nature reserve sign (centre foreground) in the dunes at Shell Bay, in a study by Colin Graham in 1985, looking north-east with Bournemouth Pier and Albany flats on the West Cliff being the notable structures on the shore and cliff top in the distance.*

# Poole Harbour

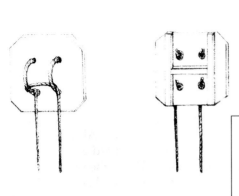

*Mud-pattens were essential for harbour boatmen before cord grass consolidated the mud-flats in the twentieth century.*

Right: *The 'Poole canoe' in 1830.*

FIG. 1, THE POOLE CANOE.

FIG. 2. THE POOLE CANOE FORESHORTENED

Left: *Old Poole canoes, or punts as we call them, on the Purbeck shore of Poole Harbour in the 1920s.*

Right: *Houseboats on Gravel Point, between South Haven Point and Bramble Bush Bay, in a low-tide photograph by Edwin Dodshon in 1927, looking south-westwards to the distant line of Purbeck Hills from Ballard Down to Nine Barrow Down (right).*

*Beached boat at South Haven Point, in a view by Edwin Dodshon in 1927, looking north-westwards across South Deep to Brownsea Island.*

colonisation by marram and Lyme grasses. The front-line dunes, beloved by nudists, are distinctly unstable and fall away to the long beach that acts as the penultimate barrier to an adverse sea. The final line of natural defence is a continuation of gradual descent with the offshore sand extending far enough to dampen the power and energy of waves and tides.

A different form of stabilisation now protects the landward side of South Haven peninsula. A series of salt marshes dates from the twentieth century. I can say that with the evidence on my desk. Victorian naturalist John Clavell Mansel-Pleydell (1817–1902) of Whatcombe House, Winterborne Whitechurch, discovered a 'single small clump' of the cord grass *Spartina townsendii* at Owre (Ower) mud-flats, Poole Harbour, on 17 July 1899. He sent a tuft of that grass, which had not been found before in Dorset, to botanist H.J. Goddard of Tottenham Road, Longfleet, Poole.

Mansel-Pleydell's 'Whatcombe Herbarium' label, which accompanied the specimen, is before me as I write. I found it inserted into Goddard's copy of the 1895 second edition of Mansel-Pleydell's *Flora of Dorsetshire* which is now in my collection of antiquarian Dorset books. Goddard went on to compile the *Grasses of Great Britain*, as a result of sustained collecting from 1875 to 1936, and worked for Dunns Farm Seeds Limited. It was Goddard who reported the spread of *Spartina townsendii*, to the other side of the harbour, in a letter published by the *Dorset County Chronicle* on 19 August 1907:

*This plant was discovered in Dorset by our late friend J.C. Mansel-Pleydell, in 1899, at Owre [Ower], Poole Harbour. I still possess a specimen which he very kindly sent me at the time. Since then I have 'kept an eye open' for it year by year but without success, when*

*The Coastguard Lookout on Studland beach, which remained operational until 1918, seen in 1900.*

this season 'all at once' it appears in hundreds of spots, in fact in nearly every mud-flat in Lytchett Bay, Lake, Holes Bay, Whitecliff, Salterns etc. and is now, instead of being 'very rare', as in Linton (Flora of Bournemouth) [1900], 'very common'.

Lord Montagu of Beaulieu gave evidence before the Royal Commission on Land Erosion in 1907. He said that there had been a similar rapid spread of cord grass – then locally known as 'sea-rice' or 'rice grass' – on the Hampshire estuaries. *Spartina townsendii* had been accidentally introduced, entangled in the anchor chains of ships from the Argentine, a couple of decades earlier. It was so rampant and invasive in its chosen environmental niche that by 1907 it was estimated to have overrun huge areas of inshore mud banks, solidifying and raising them, to cover a total area in the Solent and Southampton Water of between 6,000 and 8,000 acres. By then it was also firmly established in

Dorset. Goddard noted that 'great clumps could be counted by the thousand all around Poole Harbour on nearly every mud-flat.'

Poole Harbour pattens or mud boards were described by Colonel Peter Hawker in his 1830 work, *Guns and Shooting*. In its 1859 revised edition he admits to underestimating their size in his print showing how they are used. It gave '12 inches square' but Colonel Hawker pointed out that this should have read '16 inches square'. So make sure you note the change in the specification if you follow his instructions:

*Put your foot in C, with your heel against D; place one of the small ropes on each side of the foot, and under C; then over it, and under D. Having done this draw the ropes together, as tight as the foot can bear them, and tie them under your instep. These boards are, of necessity, larger, and fitted up with a stronger rope than the others, because the Poole ground is so very soft.*

*Looking south-eastwards across Middle Beach in 1900.*

## Studland Beach

*Middle Beach boatman with three vessels offered for hire
in 1900, in a view south-eastwards to Redend Point
(right) and Old Harry Rocks (left).*

**The rock on the beach in 1905 in a view south-eastwards
towards Old Harry Rocks.**

## *Studland Beach*

*Bloomsbury era postcards of Middle Beach in the early 1920s, showing tents, a sailing-boat, visitors and the newly-built Studland Pier beside Redend Point (top picture).*

## Studland Beach

Left: *Middle Beach in 1930, showing Studland Pier extending seawards from Redend Point.*

**Trainee yachtsmen at low water on the landward side of the Training Bank, pictured by Edwin Dodshon in 1931.**

Right: *Studland Pier and Studland Bay, photographed by Edwin Dodshon in 1931, looking eastwards to the Isle of Wight* (top left).

## Studland Beach

Left: *Middle Beach tearoom offering a window looking eastwards across Studland Bay, beyond a wind-blown sycamore in 1984.*

Below: *Sail and sand at South Beach, pictured by Colin Graham in 1984, north-westwards towards scrubby Redend Point.*

## *Studland Beach*

Above: *Studland Bay, showing an empty expanse of sand, photographed by Colin Graham in 1985 in a view southwards to Ballard Down.*

Right: *Front-line beach huts, photographed by Colin Graham in 1984, looking northwards from Middle Beach.*

# Studland Beach

Above: *Single-wicket bowler and batsman in a timeless scene on Studland beach caught by Colin Graham in July 1985.*

Below: *Studland dunes, in a view by Colin Graham in 1985, across semi-consolidated sands, north-westwards to Little Sea (far left).*

Flowering plants around Little Sea include the bog bean, marsh cinquefoil, yellow flag, and bog asphodel. The waters have eels and palmate newts and are fished by cormorants and herons. The latter breed on Brownsea Island. Dabchick and water rail breed at Little Sea. In winter it attracts large flocks of mallard, teal, wigeon and pochard, and smaller numbers of tufted duck, pintail, shoveler, coot and Bewick's swan.

All wildlife in Purbeck has its followers and surveys of the extent of Purbeck's use by naturalists show that the majority come to watch birds and the South Haven peninsula is the most visited part of the island. There, in the area shared with naturists who have established one of the best known of nudist beaches on the South Coast, is the bonus of making the chance discovery of another natural phenomenon, the elusive 'singing sands'.

Between Shell Bay and Studland, just above the high-water mark, visitors have occasionally trodden musical notes. The earliest record, in a guidebook of 1890, states that these sands, composed of rounded, polished grains mostly of quartz, occurred 'in a narrow zone varying from 12 to 15 yards between blown sand and the high-water mark.' Kathleen Green was shown these sands by Studland children in 1918:

*One patch of these sands lay about 400 yards north from the point where the lane to the Coastguard Station leads to the beach. They gave a high-pitched note... midway between the lane and the remains of an old wreck, the coarser sand under the sand dunes gave a low pitch, the finer sand on the sea side of the patch, a higher note.*

In the 1920s, S.E. Clarke was asked: 'Have you ever heard the whistling sands?' He recalled that he was led along the beach to an area where 'each footstep produced a swishing or whistling sound at a high-pitched note.' Miss M.S. Homer wrote in 1930: 'There was no doubt about it; as the foot stepped on the sand, there was a distinct note, and on striking the sand with a stick, a resonant musical sound.'

Palm trees transformed the Studland dunes into 'North Africa' in the spring of 1978 for the BBC television series 'Warship' featuring 2,600-ton Leander-class frigate HMS *Phoebe*, alias HMS *Hero* for the filming. That was done in the evening to portray a night landing. Once they had discovered the suitability and cost-effectiveness of having Studland doubling for the tropics, film crews returned many times. Comic turns included some memorable romps for 'The Benny Hill Show'.

By the end of the twentieth century, having received a vitriolic letter taking me to task for photographing an abundance of bladderwrack beside a distinctly thinning Studland beach, I was relieved to find the phenomenon listed in a National Trust report as an example of climate change:

*Following complaints from visitors, action has been taken over the summer to temporarily remove the excess seaweed deposits from Studland beach. These deposits have occurred as a result of a change in weather patterns, particularly the increase in easterly winds, causing further erosion which has narrowed the beach and concentrated the seaweed more than normal*

Left: *Little Sea, as close as you usually come to it, as the jewel of Studland Heath National Nature Reserve.*

Below: *Tranquil water, as usual, on Little Sea, in a view northwards into the South Haven peninsula in 1985.*

*Heather knolls on Godlingston Heath in a 1985 view by Colin Graham, looking north-eastwards to Brand's Bay and Brownsea Island with the South Haven peninsula and Poole Bay to the right.*

*along the three miles of sandy beach. Information boards describing the importance of seaweed to the ecology of the shoreline and the dunes have been placed on the beach.*

The Trust saved 30 beach huts 'from storms and wind' by moving them into the sheltered dip beside a wartime tank-trap north-east of Middle Beach car park. Inland, a substantial remnant of Dorset's great heath – the Egdon Heath of Thomas Hardy's novels – stretches westwards across more than half the parish to the unbroken line of conifer plantations that now mark the historic boundary line between Bankes land and the Rempstone Estate. Studland Heath National Nature Reserve, including Godlingston Heath, covers more than 1,500 acres and protects one of the last unspoilt tracts of lowland heather and bog that is large enough to remain ecologically viable and virtually self-sustainable. The flat-bottomed boggy valleys are almost featureless in the topographical sense but come to life like a blooming desert in the summer sun with a contrast of striking colours as blue marsh gentian and tufts of white cotton grass arise from florist-quality sphagnum moss.

Two of the heath's principal species are the rare and harmless smooth snake (more slender than the adder and without zig-zag markings) and its colourful sand lizard prey. Adders and common lizards are also present. Grass snakes, toads and frogs are common in the birch and sallow scrub towards Studland village and I have intervened, without harm to either party, to save a huge toad that was firmly gripped in the comparatively small mouth of a grass snake as the pair thrashed about in a stream. Above this intermediate zone is a dependable place for seeing the parrot-like flight of green woodpeckers, accompanied by the characteristic 'yaffle' cry that has given them their West-Country dialect name. 'They are the rain birds,' Leonard Tatchell used to say. 'You hear a chorus of shrieks from the trees in advance of an overnight weather front.'

*The smooth snake predator is even rarer than its sand lizard prey.*

*Adult sand lizard eating an insect.*

*Young sand lizards.*

35

# Redend Point

Left: 'Slumbering Sea' by Australia's most acclaimed artist, Tom Roberts from Dorchester, in 1887, identified as Redend Point after Rodney Legg took a reversed copy of it to the mirror.

Australian artist Tom Roberts.

Right: Exposed sandstone of Redend Point, looking south-east in 1925.

Above: South Beach with a young lady making the picture, in a view north-westwards to Redend Point in 1930.

Right: Old Harry Rocks from the north-west, photographed from the rock pools of Redend Point by Colin Graham in 1983.

Heathland birds include the Dartford warbler, distinctive with purple breast and cocky tail, which belongs now to any suitable patch of gorse scrub in Dorset, having expanded from its refuge on the Arne peninsula over the past three decades without the setback of a disastrously cold winter. The nightjar, an almost primeval-looking summer visitor, is another Studland speciality. So too are the stonechat and linnet, with the harvest mice sharing their habitat without a single stalk of grain in sight.

The other Studland landscape begins to the south of the great beach, after Redend Point, where a 50-foot cliff marks the limit of Studland's open sands. The bright variety of sandstone colours, between Middle Beach and the much smaller South Beach, were collected a century ago and sold in bottles. Across the water, no doubt giving Studland the idea, Alum Bay sand is one of the oldest of holiday souvenirs.

The best Victorian painting of Redend Point and the cliffs towards Old Harry Rocks came to light in unusual circumstances in 2002. One of Australia's finest painters was recognised as 'a poor boy from Dorset' who is now commemorated by a plaque unveiled on a terraced house in Durngate Street, Dorchester, by the Australian High Commissioner on 4 May 2002. Tom Roberts was born there in 1856, the son of the editor of the *Dorset County Chronicle*, Richard Roberts, who died in 1868. His sudden demise left widow Matilda Roberts and her three children impoverished and an appeal fund in the county town paid for them to emigrate to join relatives on the other side of the world. Tom Roberts showed immediate promise as a photographic assistant, and then did well on a design course in Melbourne. By 1881 he had the means to return to Britain and studied at the Royal Academy of Art. His seminal work, the 'Shearing of the Rams', was an instant and lasting success in capturing the essence of the new nation. It now hangs in the National Gallery of Victoria, in Adelaide, and has been reproduced on a $4 postage stamp.

As part of his belated recognition back home the *Western Daily Press* published an 1887-dated Constable-like seascape captioned 'Slumbering Sea, Mentone'. Mentone sounds like a process but is also a town name in Indiana and Texas. However, it is much nearer to Tom's home, and even closer to Studland.

As it was reproduced, however, it cannot be Studland Bay as the cliffs and rocks are the wrong way round. On taking it to a mirror, as one does if you are me, it became instantly recognisable. 'Slumbering Sea' is a view from Middle Beach, south-eastwards to Redend Point and the chalk cliffs below King Barrow, with the ridge of Ballard Down beyond. Every rock tallies with Victorian photographs. The newspaper had printed the transparency the wrong way round! Ironically, thwarting my attempts at trying to correct the error, our own printers were also initially reluctant to reverse it.

Up on the hills, from 1960 till 1990, there were few kind things to be said for the great open slope extending from the very top of Ballard Down and sweeping across to the fringes of Studland village and in places across the coast path. Firstly, there is the incongruous suburban implant of the 1930s chalets of the Glebeland Estate, set half a mile south of the village at the centre of the hillside. David Bett, Regional Director of the National Trust, told visiting members of his ruling council how it had escaped Bankes ownership:

*The story on the estate is that it was a piece of glebe pasture that was being sold by the Church Commissioners in London after the Great War.*

Left: *Captioned 'On the downs', this scrubby postcard view is northwards across a very rustic Studland in 1903.*

ON THE DOWNS, STUDLAND.

**Godlingston Hill and the Ulwell Gap in an Edwardian watercolour.**

*Charlie Battrick ploughing between King Barrow and Ballard Down on 26 October 1938, in a view looking north across Studland Bay to the South Haven peninsula.*

## Purbeck Hills

Right: *Viewpoint layby between Kingswood Farm and Currendon doing brisk business in 1973.*

Inset: *Historic boundary stone, inscribed in 1776 for 'Studland Manor', redundant as a marker now that National Trust land covers both slopes of Ballard Down.*

Main: *Ballard Down with its National Trust stile and sign in the south-west corner of Studland Parish, in the middle of the Ulwell Gap, photographed by Rodney Legg in 1994.*

Right: *'Rest and be Thankfull' (sic) on the Purbeck stone seat provided by law writer David Jardine in 1852, on top of Ballard Down.*

# Purbeck Hills

*Street gas lamp from London's Mansion House, re-erected as an obelisk on Ballard Down, photographed by John Pitfield in 1981, with the author for scale.*

*Hexagonal section of the displaced part of Ballard Down Obelisk with Colin Graham's photograph from 1985 showing the gas pipe in situ (centre).*

*Golf course, Studland Heath, Little Sea and across Studland Bay to the cliff-top landmarks of Branksome Park and Westbourne, pictured by Rodney Legg in 2002.*

*Isle of Purbeck Golf Club links eastwards to its clubhouse (top right), on National Trust heathland between Studland and the Purbeck Hills, seen in 2000.*

*The far green of the Isle of Purbeck Golf Club, towards Nine Barrow Down, proving a challenge too far for this pair of golfers in 2000.*

*Mr Bankes instructed his agent to go up and bid, which meant acquire it for whatever it made, but he is said to have missed the train and it went to a developer. Oddly, we've since been given a plot there that was never built on, and now preserve it as an oasis of orchids and downland flowers, among the bungalows.*

Post-war improvements have extended almost all of the buildings into modern luxury homes, with the bonus of a glorious view over the village and coast. Mature gardens now soften their impact.

Though the upper part of the northern slope of Ballard Down has a superb chalkland flora, with orchids and bellflowers, the rest of this landscape was converted into a vast cereal acreage, though hardly a prairie as these flinty slopes were never going to be highly productive grain land, no matter how much fertiliser and subsidies were thrown at them. The farming operation centred on Manor Farm, on the south side of Studland village, and when its tenancy fell in for re-letting in 1991 the National Trust removed 200 acres from the holding. These are being restored to natural grassland or woodland, mostly with public access, and the land retained for normal farming is being managed with traditional crop rotation and a return to dairying.

On the other side of Studland, between the western part of the village and the southern edge of Studland Heath, the Trust is also allowing a corridor of fields to revert to semi-natural pasture land as 'a quiet area' for wildlife and the comparatively few non-coastal walkers.

South-westwards, the notable landmark is a former City of London gas lamp erected as an obelisk on Ballard Down (SZ 022 813) by Swanage contractor and entrepreneur George Burt in 1892. It commemorates the opening of Ulwell Reservoir, where water was first tapped from the chalk formation in 1884, and has had an up-and-down existence. Having collapsed soon after erection, it was rebuilt, but torn down again in 1940 to prevent its use as a navigation marker for German bombers. The Luftwaffe set bearings from coastal features before heading inland on a compass bearing. It was re-erected in 1973 but is only 23 feet high – lacking a 6-foot section of white Cornish granite which is displaced beside the plinth – a gas pipe can be seen running through the centre.

Off the other end of Ballard Down and its fault-line, underwater springs are recorded by Richard Gough, who edited the second edition of Dorset's county history after the death of John Hutchins:

*On the south side of the Studland Bay, near Handfast Point or Old Harry, are three springs of fresh water, 12 feet below high-water mark, the largest of which discharges between four and five tons of water in a minute. They are within ten feet of each other and run in parallel courses.*

Studland fisherman David Sales told me that the water bubbles up in quantity and that the flow continued during the double drought years of 1975–76. A century earlier the barge men carrying stone from Swanage knew the spot and lowered casks into the sea to fill them with drinking-water. A similar spot where fishermen used to drink is known in Kimmeridge Bay.

The parish line between Studland and Swanage runs for more than a mile along the hog's back spine of Ballard Down, from the slopes of Ulwell Gap in the west to the exposed chalk of Ballard Cliff in the east, where the boundary drops southwards and seawards to give Ballard Head or Point to Studland. With National Trust land on either side, the barbed-wire fence became redundant, and has been removed to restore the open landscape of the former open sheep-leaze. The summit boundary, a distance of 2,500 yards, is marked by eight eighteenth-century marker stones which are cut on the north-facing side with 'S M' for Studland Manor.

The penultimate stone from the east, 250 yards west from the main cluster of Bronze-Age round barrows (SZ 038 813), is dated 1776. Swanage Public Bridleway No. 6 follows the south side of this boundary and passes all the stones (from SZ 021 813 in the west to SZ 040 813 in the east). The stone Judge's Seat, with a 'Rest and be Thankfull' (sic) inscription, beside the public path up and over the hill (SZ 034 813), on the Studland side of the parish line, was provided in 1852 by legal author David Jardine (1794–1860). As the Recorder for Bath, who came from Weybridge, he had adopted Swanage and provided a matching seat on Peveril Down.

# Chapter 3

# PREHISTORIC & ROMAN TIMES

*The Ulwell Barrow, photographed by Colin Graham from the Studland side, with a London gas-lamp obelisk rising at the edge of the Bronze-Age burial mound in Swanage Parish.*

The earliest archaeological remains in the Studland landscape are its share of Dorset's 2,000-plus ancient burial mounds. Positioned on or below the Purbeck Hills they must include examples from the rich and aristocratic Wessex Culture of the Bronze Age. Dating from 2100BC to 1500BC it is credited with the final development of Stonehenge. A total of 18 definite burial mounds are recorded from Studland Parish with four of them being shared as boundary markers with Swanage. The following examples which I have chosen to mention are those distinguished by a name.

## Ballard Down Barrows
### (SZ 027 812)

Three of five bowl-type Bronze-Age burial mounds inside the 500-feet contour on the spine of the hill, in a line from west to east that marks the parish boundary between Studland and Swanage. Each is now reduced

to a hump, having been disturbed by wartime trenches and buildings and subsequently spread by ploughing, though the National Trust has now restored the area to chalk grassland.

## Cracker Barrow
### (SZ 035 817)

A Bronze-Age mound, standing to the west of the Glebeland estate, below the northern slope of Ballard Down. It gave its name to Cracker Barrow Furlong of the medieval strip fields and was eventually destroyed by ploughing.

## Fishing Barrow
### (SZ 018 821)

A Bronze-Age bell-shaped burial mound, of somewhat modified form as its top was scalped and flatted for a golf tee. The 9-feet high mound is 99 feet in diameter, including traces of a berm sloping towards the ditch.

The latter is 23 feet wide and nearly 2 feet deep, which at times has held water, and hence the name.

## King Barrow
### (SZ 046 820)

This Bronze-Age bowl-shaped burial mound from about 1800BC, is 45 feet in diameter and 4 feet high. It lies on the chalk foothills midway between Studland village and Ballard Down, in an unploughed corner of the fields 250 yards east of Warren Wood. The mound was opened at the centre by antiquaries but the results went unrecorded.

## Kingswood Farm Barrows
### (SZ 007 820)

Three Bronze-Age bell-type burial mounds and a smaller bowl-type mound, down to the north-east of the viewpoint layby overlooking Godlingston Heath. The biggest bell barrow is 58 feet in diameter and 4 feet high, surrounded by a flat berm 8 feet wide, and an outer ditch 11 feet wide and 2 feet deep. There is an excavation pit at the top. Beside it is another bell barrow, 56 feet in diameter and 3 feet high with a berm 12 feet wide, plus a ditch 12 feet wide and nearly 2 feet deep. The other mounds are less distinctive.

## Studland Bay House Barrows
### (SZ 033 830)

A Bronze-Age burial mound, 46 feet in diameter and 6 feet high, in the front garden of the house. The eastern half has been removed. There is another mound to the north-west, across the road, in the field towards Knoll House Hotel.

## Thorny Barrow
### (SZ 014 821)

A Bronze-Age bowl-type barrow, apparently, about 65 feet in diameter and 8 feet high, though eroded by a sandpit.

## Ulwell Barrow
### (SZ 022 813)

A Bronze-Age bowl-shaped mound, 75 feet in diameter and 6 feet high on Swanage Parish boundary at the western end of Ballard Down. It is notable for the obelisk, an old London gas standard, built into its southern side in 1892 to commemorate abstraction 'of pure water from the chalk formation'. Victorian antiquary John Austen excavated a primary Bronze-Age inhumation in a chalk-cut grave, with the crouched burial having been provided with a fine cup with handles in red-ware, for the warrior's trip to the afterlife. Flat stones surrounded the skull and antler fragments occurred in the filling. Near the centre of the mound were the 'disunited' bones of another skeleton, fragments of urns, and a later cremation under a stone at a higher level. There were also flint fragments and Iron-Age or Romano-British pot sherds and disturbance towards the top of the barrow.

## Early Settlements

Ancient fields cover at least 65 acres between Ballard Down and Handfast Point (SZ 040 820). They date from the Iron Age and Romano-British period. Further areas, between the four main mapable blocks, were obliterated by medieval ploughing. Almost all traces above ground were flattened by late-twentieth-century ploughing. Until then the best preserved group was a 12-acre block of small enclosures varying from square shapes to rectangles stretching up the slope on the northern side of Ballard Down (SZ 035 815). Some of the lynchets were 8 feet high. The contemporary access route was a banked trackway that approached from lower ground to the south-east and ran diagonally up through the enclosures until being blocked on the 400-feet contour by the 2-feet-high scarp-line of the southern-most field. This track indicates that the probable location of one of the adjacent ancient settlements of native farmers is covered by Warren Wood (SZ 043 821).

Woodhouse Hill Roman Buildings (SZ 031 822) comprise a large group of rooms and courtyards covering a substantial area, upwards of 1,600 yards, which is the size of a modern farm. They lie across the eastern part of the wood on Woodhouse Hill. Two clusters of heath-stone and flint foundations were uncovered by Norman Field between 1952 and 1958. The stone walls were up to 3 feet thick and probably supported cob walls. The site had a long life and was most likely still occupied in the early-fourth century. The northern room, at least, was built at that time as it had a coin of the British usurper Allectus, dated to 293–96, beneath the floor. The next building had five coins from the second half of the third century (259–96). South of this building were the remains of a much earlier circular hut which had been flanked with sheds on all sides. A Samian platter, a high-quality import, lay on a low clay shelf on the west side, and was dated to AD65–80. There was also a coin of Vespasian (AD73) and crucibles for bronze-working. Lesser remains of a similar hut and workshops were found south of the entrance to the later building to the east. The main southern group of buildings, 80 feet closer to the road, also had a long and complicated history. Underlying the east-west rectangles of third-century buildings was a room of the late-first century AD, aligned north-west to south-east. Three fossil sea urchins were found during the course of the excavation, each in a different room, which may be more than coincidental. They have also been recorded from Bronze-Age graves and may have been regarded as sun symbols because of their shape and radiating lines.

There was an extensive Roman cemetery around St Nicholas Parish Church (SZ 036 825). Archaeologist J. Bernard Calkin, a retired headmaster from Langton Matravers, adopted me on my visits to the Red House Museum at Christchurch in 1961 and gave me my first antiquities. He opened boxes of

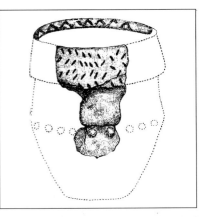

*Bronze-Age pottery excavated by John Austen in June 1857 from the round barrow above Ulwell Gap at the western end of Ballard Down.*

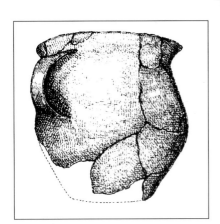

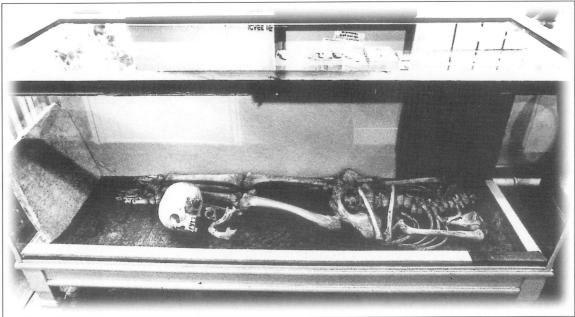

Above: *The Roman burial discovered in 1951 beside Studland Parish Church, reassembled in the Red House Museum at Christchurch, photographed by Colin Graham in 1984.*

Below: *Detail of the Romano-British female from Studland, showing her feet and decapitated skull with detached lower jaw.*

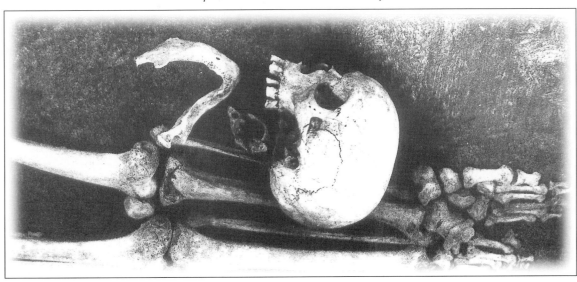

Studland finds and told me that William Masters Hardy, a Swanage builder and antiquary, had found numerous stone cists and a rotary quern when restoring St Nicholas Church in 1881. Others were found in the churchyard extension, on the 100-feet contour, during the first half of the twentieth century. Complete cists of Purbeck marble, floored with stone, were found in 1951 and 1955.

The finds he was working on came from the 1951 discovery which was a skeleton laid in a pagan alignment with the upper part of the body at the south-east and the feet towards the north-west. The gravedigger came upon the cist, beside the church wall, and called in the schoolmaster to excavate the burial. Bernard Calkin referred to 'the forensic report' from pathologist Professor John Cameron and told me:

*She was a lady aged about 35 to 40. The Kimmeridge shale spindle-whorl was placed on the pelvis, but what was remarkable was that she had been decapitated, with the severed head and detached mandible placed beside the left foot. It wasn't an execution, because that was done after death, and the burial was carried out with care and respect. Nor was it removed so that the body would fit because there would have been more than three inches to spare if the head had been left in place. I am sure that she was mentally disturbed and that the head was detached to quieten her spirit.*

Calkin and the sexton also retrieved a single cockleshell from the grave before its precarious sides began to collapse. In 1947 he had excavated a similar grave at Kimmeridge which was dated to the end of the third century by a coin of Carausius. This female also had a shale spindle-whorl near the left hand. Her detached lower jaw and severed head lay between the left knee and ankle. Food had been provided for the afterlife:

*She was much older, plump and toothless, suffering from severe arthritis in the hips. We also know of trussed-up barrow burials from the Purbeck Hills. I am sure that in the case of Romano-British females they were bad-tempered gossiping grandmas who had their tongues removed after death to prevent them chattering in the next world. They were given the spindle-whorl for something useful to do. As a long-standing Purbeck folk-memory it explains the Silent Woman, the inn name at Coldharbour, near Wareham. The sign shows her carrying her head.*

William Masters Hardy, the builder who saved St Nicholas Parish Church from collapse in 1881, dug deep into the footings and recorded earlier masonry as well as the series of stone cists:

*In the old foundations were bedded massive stone*

*steps, rudely axed, with mortised holes, about four inch square, to admit the door-jambs – evidently non-ecclesiastical – evidently remains from some very ancient village, Saxon holding, or strong keep, worked out of local sandstone of the consistence of the hoary and lonely Agglestone Rock on the heath. Also a huge keystone of an arch, suitable for a radius of five feet, was turned up; likewise a hand-mill formed by two round stones about 18 inches in diameter, one of them having a hole at its centre.*

Dozens of mystery circles, perhaps associated with salt-panning, lie in dense clusters on the north-west side of the Ferry Road between Redhorn Quay and Jerry's Point (SZ 025 855 to 029 860). A total of 71 have been mapped across the heathland. Six more are on similar terrain immediately south of the track to Greenland Farm (SZ 021 845). Others lay to the south-west but have been ploughed for pasture. The Royal Commission on Historical Monuments notes that the highest lies at 32 feet above sea-level and that their size varies from 9 to 27 feet across. They form irregular circles with each being surrounded by a bank about a foot in height. The interiors of these earthworks are 'slightly dished but all are almost horizontal, being built up downhill and cut back uphill if on the slight slope to the harbour'. Some hold bog flora and two deeper examples may have been ponds. Their date could be anywhere between the Iron Age and AD1700. Thirteen low sandy mounds 'have also defied explanation', as has a line of five stones, regularly placed and originally upright, set from south to north across the middle of the peninsula between Brand's Bay and Little Sea. A sixth stone lies 100 yards north-west, towards Redhorn Quay.

The Domesday survey of 1086 records that the Count of Mortain, half-brother of King William the Conqueror, owned 32 'saline' – salt-pans – at Studland. They were valued at 40 shillings, which was significant as a quarter of the total manorial assets, and another 13 salt-pans, owned by Milton Abbey, lay to the west at Ower. The next place in that direction, Wytch, owes its name to salt extraction and sale, as do Nantwich in Cheshire and Ipswich in Suffolk. The University of London commentary on the Dorset section of the Domesday Book notes the mention of 'plumba' at Arne for leaden vessels used in boiling the sea water to collect the salt. There the salt-pans were owned by Shaftesbury Abbey and a second survey, in the twelfth century, confirms the existence of a hide of land used exclusively for the production of salt. The far arm of Poole Harbour, north of Bank Gate Cottages beside the Wareham Channel, has yielded extensive evidence of earlier salt-pans. Roman briquetage, the brick-like remains of clay containers, was found strewn across the ground when it was being ploughed for conifer planting.

# Chapter 4

# CHURCH, CROSS & CASTLE

*1820: from the south-west, by Julia M. Colson.*

The Parish Church of St Nicholas in Studland village competes with St Martin's in Wareham for the accolade of being the oldest complete church in Dorset. Studland's church was 'probably built shortly before the Conquest' according to the Royal Commission on Historical Monuments. That was the Norman Conquest of 1066, placing the likely date in the reign of the last of the Saxon monarchs, King Harold. The Commission's use of the word 'probably' does not rule out a slightly later date, in the opening years of the reign of William the Conqueror. The chancel and central tower are original but the nave was rebuilt in the late-eleventh century, though on its original foundations, making the church a national rarity as a surviving fusion of late-Saxon and early-Norman architecture. The font, a simple convex-sided stone bowl mounted on an original window-head, is contemporary. The tower has always looked more quaint and venerable than the makers intended, as

Norman work to add six feet to the top stage had to be abandoned when supporting arches threatened to burst, explaining why it was hastily finished off with low gables. More work was accomplished a little later, but otherwise St Nicholas has remained in its time warp, as the Commission concludes in its 1970 report:

*The church is an interesting example of mid-twelfth-century elaboration of a comparatively small and simple pre-Conquest church. The building has a solid robustness of character which is impressive.*

Architectural historian Fred Pitfield, whose *Purbeck Parish Churches* was published in 1985, points out that there are 'only a dozen or so complete or near complete Norman village churches in England'. Moreover, he continues, the Norman work at Studland 'is built around the core of the still earlier pre-Conquest structure.' He credits rector Revd C.R.

45

# Studland Church

Left: *1820: from the south-east, by Julia M. Colson.*

Right: *1853: interior, eastwards from the font, by Frederick Leigh Colvile.*

Left: *1853: from the south-west, with columnar cypress trees making their debut in an ink-and-wash sketch by C.M. Colvile.*

Right: *1853: from the south, by C.M. Colvile.*

## *Studland Church*

*1892: newly restored and braced tower arches, looking north-eastwards towards the altar, photographer unknown.*

*1900: from the south-west, photographer unknown.*

Digby, enlightened Victorian diocesan architect George Crickmay, from Weymouth, and Swanage builder William Masters Hardy for a careful and meticulously recorded restoration in 1881. This preserved rather than rebuilt the ancient fabric.

The newly-formed Society for the Protection of Ancient Buildings successfully urged sympathetic treatment when the building was in danger 'from a threatened and utter collapse' after 'immense cracks' developed in the walls and tower arches. Even a buttress, provided in 1840, was doing more harm than good as it had been placed directly above a lead coffin. As the coffin bulged the buttress began to pull the wall further out of line. It was a miracle that these defects were righted by the light touch, forbidding any hammering of the arches, pushing in concrete and iron supports rather than commissioning the radical rebuilding that was so often seen as the only fashionable solution. Floors were returned to their original levels and tombstones replaced in their correct positions. Red and blue frescoes, of a standing male figure with one kneeling at either side, were revealed beneath whitewash and plaster. Remarkable in itself, this retention of the general integrity of the early fabric has provided us with other evidence of Studland's former ecclesiastical status. Mr Pitfield is in no doubt that St

Nicholas was a minster rather than just another village church:

*In view of the Saxon origin and the quality and extent of the subsequent Norman work, it was evidently a church of some importance during the eleventh and twelfth centuries, and was in all probability a Minster church serving an area covering the eastern part of Purbeck approximating to the Domesday hundred of Aylswood. In most other cases villages or towns associated with Minster churches have grown considerably, accompanied by a comparable growth in the church itself, but Studland has retained its small village character over the centuries, so that its ancient church has survived practically in its original state.*

The work includes the full Norman details of corbeltables, windows, doorways, arches and vaulting. The arches supporting the tower are superb, incorporating two styles, as the inner roll is moulded on the underside, and the outer roll is moulded on the west-facing angles. They spring from rounded respond shafts with scalloped capitals. Simple ornamentation includes chevrons, zig-zag lines below with semi-circular toppings, and springing stars and hatching. William Masters Hardy, who knew his Purbeck stone as well

# Studland Church

*1907: from the south-west, with conifers in their prime, in a watercolour by Sidney Heath.*

# Studland Church

1908: interior, eastwards to the altar, by Thomas Powell.

1948: lectern, organ and cracked corner of tower arch, photographer unknown.

Right: 1974: from the south-east, by Colin Graham.

Below: 1983: from the south, by Colin Graham.

# Studland Church

*1983: from the south-west, by Colin Graham.*

Above: *1985: nave seating and rafters, eastwards from the gallery, by Colin Graham.*

Left: *1983: from the south-east, by Colin Graham.*

Four pictures on this page: *The Norman corbel-table, with one or two heads and fabulous beasts in detail, photographed by Rodney Legg in 2002.*

as anyone, confidently identified its source:

*The groins are of Purbeck burr and soft enough to be carved with a knife, wondrously light for such architecture, being porous; the burr is unfitted for facing. The stone can be obtained only from rocks which appear at low tide 30 yards east of the stone quay at Swanage. There are no other arches in the neighbourhood turned with this stone. A proper radiation has been maintained of the stones in the arches.*

Corbels on the west side of the chancel arch would have supported a medieval rood beam. Cuts in the east side of the chancel arch and to the upper parts of the responds and adjacent vaulting shafts show that it supported a rood gallery.

The gallery dates from the late-eighteenth century with a replacement oak front dating from 1910. In the unexpected coronation year of King George VI and Queen Elizabeth in 1937, after Edward VIII's abdication, Sir Herbert Cook presented the church with an organ. Made by Hill, Norman and Beard, it was originally placed on the north side of the chancel, but had to be moved in 1960 to enable repair and pointing of the masonry. It was put 'in the west end above the gallery, electrically connected to the console, which remained in the chancel.'

Outside, the Norman corbel-table is the best of its kind in the county, with a variety of geometric ornaments, human heads and grotesque and fabulous beasts. Even the oldest and biggest of the four bells – 'showing fire-cracks and sounding ill' – comes into the frame, though it has been derided as something of a fraud. The date '1065' and 'Draw nigh to God' are an unlikely combination of Arabic numerals and English inscription. The answer might be that the zero and six were transposed during the casting and the date should have been given as 1605. On the other hand it is quite a coincidence that 1065 should be the most likely year for the building of the tower.

There is further confusion for the accolade of the

*This page and overleaf: Treleven Haysom at work in St Aldhelm's Quarry in 1975, and on the cross-shaft mounted on its Saxon base in Studland.*

oldest parish possession. The earliest treasure has been claimed as a Coptic processional cross from sixth-century Christian Egypt, though it came as a gift from a parishioner rather than having local connections. The residual inscription is partly decipherable and was allegedly translated as follows by the British Museum:

*This is the cross of ...*
*Blessed be his seed.*
*Who gave it to Mary,*
*the daughter of ...*

The Royal Commission for Historic Monuments also looked at the lozenge-shaped brass plate, remounted on a modern staff, and identified the words as 'beginning in Geez and ending in Amharic'. Dating, the Commission says, from the nineteenth century, it was 'said to have been brought from the chapel of King Theodore of Abyssinia at Magdala in 1868.' The report goes on to give a rather different translation:

*This is the cross*
*of the chief merchant*
*Baroch Zaro.*

What is genuinely local is the gritty heath-stone plinth of the wayside cross between St Nicholas Church and Manor Farm. It is Saxon and is the only ancient cross base to have survived in the Isle of Purbeck. When I first searched it out on a grassy bank its dimensions were '4 feet in diameter and 2 feet high with a socket hole (2 feet square around a circular depression a foot deep).' The shape of this hole indicated it had supported the post of a wooden cross.

Its replacement is a masterpiece, carved in Purbeck stone at St Aldhelm's quarry, half a mile north of St Alban's Head, by sculptor Treleven Haysom. First he researched the subject of Saxon crosses – he travelled to various sites in order to 'feel the style' of surviving fragments 'to flesh-out the photographs we had been sent by the Victoria and Albert Museum'. The village would have a bargain for his £600 fee. Not only did this

include the stone but the quarrymen also took the ancient cross mound in hand, removing an overhead power line and re-routing it underground, providing a fence and hedge, then laying a gravel path around the side of the hump. The Bishop of Salisbury, Dr George Reindorp, came to Studland on 24 July 1975 to consecrate the cross, but not its elaborate carvings. They were not on it at the time, for the cross was incomplete; 12 feet high and with the actual cross at the top, but not yet carved. Canon Douglas O'Hanlon, the rector since 1972, explained to me the reason for the dummy run:

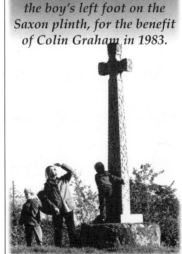

*Ancient and modern, with the boy's left foot on the Saxon plinth, for the benefit of Colin Graham in 1983.*

*We asked the Bishop to come to the village and dedicate the cross about six months ago but we were not able to give the order to the quarry in time for it to be completed. It was something of an embarrassment and I didn't want to put the ceremony off, so we decided to have the cross blessed in its blank state. A mechanical digger put it onto the Saxon ironstone base – in fact it was a good practice run for setting it in place permanently – and then plaster was poured in to hold it steady. Nothing else held it, apart from its own weight, and we were terrified that someone would lean against it. I had it surrounded by a ring of choirboys to ensure that no one got near! Then, after the ceremony it was taken back for carving and came back to us a few months later.*

The theme of the second Studland cross, a full millennium after the first, is 'Spaceship Earth' – including a supersonic airliner – scrolled Saxon-style.

The iconography embraces science and war as well as symbols of life. Growing out of primitive ears of wheat is one of the first representations in stone of the newly discovered DNA double-helix. Proceeding up the east-facing side are a violin, bomb, Concorde, butterfly and Christ, surmounted by the out strands entwining in a cross. Hell faces north and the south side spells out, 'I created this world and I sustain this world' in Dark-Age runes.

Studland Castle, a mile east of Manor Farm, stood at the far point on the promontory and jutted north-eastwards of the present Old Harry Rocks (SZ 056 826). The early-medieval Studland Castle was replaced by a blockhouse in about 1540, as one of Henry VIII's chain of coastal forts built to protect England from continental retaliation after his schism with the Catholic Church.

A similar fort is entombed, virtually intact, in the basement laundry of Branksea Castle on Brownsea Island. Together the two fortresses covered the entrance into Poole Harbour and its seaward approach along the Swash Channel. The latter is two miles due north of Old Harry Rocks. Both this Studland Castle fort and the earlier castle 'upon which it abuteth' were still visible, though out of use, when Thomas Gerard compiled his *Survey of Dorsetshire* in the 1620s. Bits of both were already falling over the cliff and they were completely washed away by 1770.

# Chapter 5
# NEWTON & GOATHORN

*Newton Bay and Goathorn Plantation, in a view from above Ower Farm eastwards across oil exploration compounds to the entrance into Poole Harbour (behind the oil rig) in 1995.*

The King's land in Purbeck, a royal warren with its fortress residence at Corfe Castle and hunting lodges in the countryside, was selected for an ambitious development project in 1286. Newton is the place name that survives at Newton Cottage (SZ 005 851) with Newton Bay to the north, in Poole Harbour, and Newton Heath stretching southwards. It was chosen for building 'a new town' and port as the enabling document authorised by Edward I makes clear:

*Appointment of Richard de Bosco... to lay out, with sufficient streets and lanes and adequate sites for a market and church and plots for merchants and others, a new town with a harbour in a place called*

*Gotowre super Mare, in the parish of Stodland [Studland] and on the King's lands... the lands and tenements of which new town the King is prepared to commit to merchants and others willing to take them and to enfeoff them thereof for building and dwelling purposes.*

'Gotowre' survives as a place name, along the Goathorn peninsula, with Ower Quay to the west where Purbeck marble was shipped through the Middle Ages for the nation's cathedral building and effigies. Though the actual site of Newton is deserted, apart from the cottage, the name still attaches to so much ground that it indicates that something was built.

Otherwise it is a name for nothing and nowhere. The Royal Commission on Historical Monuments failed to find any trace of it, but years ago, exploring when a child in 1960, I noted 'the low ruins of a collapsed stone building, apparently a church, beside a track from Greenland.'

Unfortunately, I failed to note its precise location and did not measure it, and I cannot recall what led me to think it had an ecclesiastical origin. House footings and other settlement remains lie in a shallow valley, among numerous oaks, a short distance west of the former Goathorn Railway at the south end of the peninsula. Fresh water passes along a ditch beside the house. Another structure is marked by clayey banks and the Royal Commission has dated an oak tree standing there to the year 1625. As the likely date they give to these remains is the seventeenth century there is no direct connection with Edward's new town. Yet Newton is named and marked by the symbol for a settlement on a map of 1597 so there is evidence that something was built at an earlier stage.

The scheme hardly stood much of a chance. Despite the choice of Ower Quay for the export of Purbeck marble, pulled on sledges across the heath from Corfe Castle, there was little incentive for merchants to move to an otherwise uninhabited backwater cut off from the mainland of Dorset. Newton Bay is shallow and any quay would soon have silted up.

In late-Victorian times, Newton Clay Works opened up the heathland to the south, with its story being told to Poole historian H.P. Smith by James Churchill. Born in about 1845, at Ower Quay, he married Jane Batter from Claywell, a mile away on the stream that skirts Rempstone Heath. Churchill worked for 40 years at Newton Clay Works. His wage was 12 shillings a week but from piece-work rather than a salary. His task was to remove the top covering of heathland vegetation and sand. A square area with sides of 20 feet would be excavated. On reaching the clay seam, seven 'rubblers' would take over as a gang – what we would call a team – and cut it into lumps. Depending on their personal strength they worked in two standard sizes. Chunks were either seven or eight inches wide by nine inches deep. Their spades weighed 25 pounds and had straight handles with blades six inches wide. They would only last a couple of years at Newton, because of the abrasive nature of the sand particles, whereas in the main clay pits at Norden they would survive 20 years and a man might have only two spades in his working life.

James Churchill worked at Newton before the arrival of its steam railway from Norden. They had horses to haul the clay trucks along a tramway to Goathorn Pier. Rent day for Churchill was the first Wednesday in October when the annual dues of £4.10s. had to be paid at Rempstone Hall. To sweeten the pill, Lady Caroline Calcraft provided them with a feast, but it was always a struggle to gather the required sum. 'The pig helped pay the rent,' Churchill said. 'It was bought for 25 shillings and fattened for killing a little before rent-day.' One half was cured and sold in Poole. The remainder was kept at the cottage for the winter. The Churchills also had a cow and a heifer, 36 chickens, and six ducks. They also went shooting for wildfowl when flocks of geese came south to the marshes ahead of the Arctic winds. The percussion cap gun would be punt-mounted in the boat kept below the landward end of the pier, with the vessel meeting the distinctive description for a Poole Harbour canoe as given by Colonel Peter Hawker in 1830:

*Newton Cottages, between the pines of Goathorn and the sandy fields towards Ower, mark the site of a failed medieval new town.*

*Goathorn Pier and the South Deep at high water in the 1920s, looking north-eastwards with Brownsea Island behind.*

*The Poole canoe is built sharp at both ends, on the plan of the Greenland whale-boat, except being so flat on the bottom as to draw but about two inches of water, and so light as to weigh only from 60 to 100 pounds. Dimensions – from stem to stern, 12 feet; length of bottom, 10 feet; bottom, at centre, 3 feet 2 inches; width at ditto, from gunwale to gunwale, 3 feet 7 inches; height, 11 inches at centre, rising to 13 inches fore and aft. Timbers yew or oak. Bottom to be three pieces of elm or pine an inch thick. Each side to be one plank of elm, one third of an inch thick. Caulk the seams with oakum. Then pour in hot rosin, softened with a little oil to prevent it from cracking, and paint the bottom (outside) with red lead.*

The Churchills also subsidised their income by exercising a common land right of turbary to cut 3,000 turves for fuel on the heath each year. This was done with a 'Wareham' spade which James Churchill demonstrated to H.P. Smith. Designed for peat-cutting it had a main blade a foot deep, with a flat section 7 inches wide, mainly to the right of the shaft. The left edge of this blade was bent upwards, at 90 degrees, for a 2-inch spur to do the cut to the side. Turves were detached with pressure from the right foot and then swung in that direction.

For this kind of work a dozen children came in handy. One son, Tom Churchill, described being sent to Russel Quay at Arne where the turves were about two feet by one foot and a foot thick, of a 'pethy' or peaty consistency. He was paid half a crown per thousand to cut them in May and June, and leave them to dry till September. They were then gathered into a 'turf-pook' in the shape of a beehive.

Other winter fuel for free, from the heath, included furze-faggots from gorse bushes which were gathered into 'nitches' (bundles) for 'baiting' (stoking) brick-domed bread ovens beside open fireplaces. This was done with a 'pale' (peel), a long-handled wooden baker's shovel, and the wooden door was sealed with damp clothes. Poorer neighbours, the heath-croppers, were said to use cow dung instead. Seven 6lb loaves were baked at a time with a few cakes as well. Outside the cottage was half an acre of land cultivated for potatoes and a little corn. The 'droshin' (threshing) was done by laying a sail on the ground and strewing it with corn. Two sticks, each seven feet long, were fastened together with leather for the flail. The 'wimming' (winnowing) was done with a garden sieve.

'Blackstalks' were faggots of burnt furze gathered after the gorse had been cleared by 'swailin' (burning) in April, to encourage growth of grass for grazing cattle. A 'vuzz-hook' was used and each 'nitch' weighed a hundredweight. 'We carried them with a crocked stick over the shoulder,' Tom Churchill said. Fern was also cut for animal feed on Green Island and brought to the mainland stacked across two canoes that had been tied together. 'We also took the boats round into Studland Bay,' Tom added, 'to collect seaweed for the vegetable garden.'

Fish was provided by Tom's uncles, the Harris brothers living at Ower Quay, who became the first operators of the floating bridge from Shell Bay in 1926.

For Goathorn peninsula the busiest time in its existence was the twentieth century. From 1905, with the building of the Goathorn Railway across the heath from the old Fayle's Tramway plateway at Norden at its unusual 3-feet 9-inch gauge, to 1999 when the main oil rig was dismantled, mineral extraction has been big business. Hundreds of acres of Newton Heath were dug for ball clay in the first half of the century and the main long-distance oil pipes, reaching below the entirety of Studland Parish and deep under Poole Harbour, completed the story in the last quarter.

Newton Clay Works had its own wharf a mile to the north at Goathorn Pier (SZ 016 863). This extended northwards, for 250 feet, to South Deep which is the principal channel through the backwaters of Poole Harbour. The main sheds for the locomotives of Goathorn Railway, the Victorian *Tiny* and new engine, *Thames*, were at Eldon Sidings, to the west of the Corfe River at Norden. From here the track of the Goathorn Railway crossed the small river and passed through little fields on the edge of the heath to Bushey where it ran to the north of Thrasher's Cottage – since demolished – and then stretched eastwards across the wastes of Brenscombe, Claywell and Newton. The operations for clay and oil literally overlap with the line now being the main artery for oil-exploration traffic and

# Engines of Industry

Above: Tertius, *built in 1886, was the third locomotive to work the clay-pits around Furzebrook.*

Left: Tiny *setting off from Norden with clay wagons on the six-mile line to Goathorn.*

Right: Tiny, *built at Poole in 1868, was in use at Norden clay-pits and then across to Goathorn until 1948.*

# *Wagons Roll*

Below: *Side-tipping steel clay wagon.*

Above: *'Oporto' tanker wagon which collected drinking-water, for Newton and Goathorn, from a supply near Arfleet Mill.*

Right: *Maximising the gauge with an adapted truck at the weathering beds, before the clay was processed.*

Left: *End of the line for one of the wooden wagons, which were replaced by steel trucks in the 1950s.*

*Goathorn train, stopping for a photo-call in the trees, at a level crossing near Bushey.*

doubling as a fire-break between the post-war conifer plantations of Purbeck Forest. At the east end of the woods, where the line goes into a sandy cutting through a remnant of the heath, there are traces of a siding and a limeworks. These have been subsequently smothered by wind-sown pines. A pottery ridge-tile from Goathorn, now displayed in the Town Hall Museum at Corfe Castle, is incised with a Nonconformist plea in rustic phrasing: 'Be not a bigot against no denomination.'

The railway had about 24 wagons and an improvised coach that was used from 1921 to 1939 to take the clay-workers' children from Newton and Goathorn to school in Corfe Castle. The passenger wagon had a corrugated-iron roof and was described as 'the hen-house'. A slit between the sides and the roof provided more air than light during the 20-minute journey. Progress along the line was punctuated by frequent stops to open gates at Goathorn hamlet, Churchill's Green, Fir Glen, Meadus's Lane and Thrasher's Lane.

*The school train from Goathorn to Corfe, showing the 'Hen-house' (on the left).*

The last stop for the children was at Arfleet, from where they had to walk half a mile southwards, into Corfe.

Drinking-water for the small community was imported by train in a large barrel labelled 'Oporto'. This was taken on board to the north of Corfe Waterworks, between Arfleet and Meadus's Lane, which leads to Flashetts.

On several occasions the railway was used to transport Purbeck stone. The biggest project lasted for several years, from 1928 to 1934, for the building of the mile-long spit extending south-eastwards into the sea from the eastern side of Shell Bay, to protect the Swash Channel entrance to Poole Harbour.

Known as the Training Bank, this was devised to direct the high tides into the mouth of Poole Harbour, and scour its sediment. For its building, each train had ten trucks, with three tons of stone in each. From Goathorn Pier the stone was taken out at high tide and dumped from ships to form the middle core of the breakwater. These loads settled on 10-ton blocks which had been lowered from barges to form the foundations.

The last of the old sailing vessels that came into Poole Harbour included graceful wooden vessels from Italy which arrived to collect ball clay. Among these were the barquentine *Patria* and brigantine *Auvenire*, in the 1920s, from Savona. W.H. Froud from Poole recalled the clay industry at Goathorn and Newton for me, in 1969:

*The Dorset Iron Foundry used to look after Fayle's two locomotives and my father and grandfather worked on them regularly. On some occasions in the years before 1914 I went to Goathorn with them. In those days the pier was regularly used for steamers that called to take*

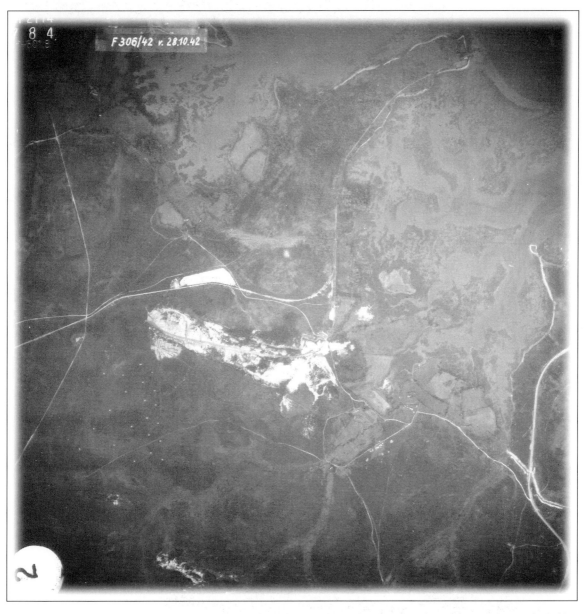

*Newton claypits, at the southern end of Goathorn peninsula, with its railway stretching westwards* (left) *and anti-invasion defences across the Ferry Road* (bottom right) *in a Luftwaffe reconnaissance photograph of 1942.*

*the clay to London. They were generally Henry Burden's boats from Poole.*

*There was one cottage at the pier, then occupied by the foreman, William Tubbs. This has now been modernised. The hamlet of Goathorn consisted of a number of cottages occupied by workers at Newton Clay Works, a small school, and a locomotive shed. There was a resident schoolmistress and the school was attended by the small number of children who lived at Goathorn. On Sunday afternoons a church service was conducted in the school by a visiting parson and organist from Swanage. The only communication with the outside world, except by boat, was along the railway to Corfe Castle and I believe that on Saturdays the people were taken on the railway for shopping – and the nearest public house.*

*The ships ceased to call at Goathorn Pier in 1930 but the works continued for some years longer. After the school was closed, because of the decline in the numbers of children, the remaining ones were taken to Corfe on the railway. One of the wagons was covered in, as a passenger coach, and Dorset County Council had to pay the clay company for the service. The hamlet and works, together with the railway, were abandoned by 1939.*

Mrs Harriet Harris, who was evacuated from Goathorn during the military occupation of 1940, moved into the village at Studland to live with her sister, Cis Green. She talked of her early-morning walks, after having killed and plucked a couple of cockerels, carrying them across heath and hills to take them to a Swanage hotel or boarding-house. That was

a ten-mile round trip. Mrs Harris had the distinction of becoming the village's oldest inhabitant. At the age of 102 she could still open and read her own post, aloud to her daughter, but one day she puzzled over the handwriting and asked Cis, 'You please give me my glasses to see if I've read it right.' Having kept her faculties until the end, she slipped away with bronchial fever at 103 years and six months.

When the evangelist Revd Brian Hession returned to a chalet beside Goathorn beach at the end of the Second World War, he came and went by boat and talked of the peninsula as 'my island'. He brought international attention to his chosen location with 'A Letter from Goathorn', filmed by the Dawn Trust, in 1948. It was presented as make-believe correspondence with an American GI named Stirling who he befriended during the war when the United States 1st Infantry Division prepared for the invasion of Europe. He gave a pen picture of his life at Goathorn:

*The only real approach is by sea. Deep water channels come right up to the point which makes it an ideal place for sailing. This is one of those favoured places in England where the climate is mild. Autumn lingers on till Christmas. Winter is only distinguishable for occasional bouts of temper which are soon forgotten.*

His only daily visitor was the water-postman who set off from Poole Quay on a circuit that included islands, houseboats, visiting ships at anchor, and a few other isolated spots along the southern shore. Leisure boats of all sorts of shape and size were already beginning to

*The chalet in the pines at Goathorn, photographed from Poole Harbour by Colin Graham in 1985.*

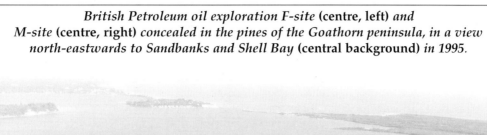

*British Petroleum oil exploration F-site* **(centre, left)** *and*
*M-site* **(centre, right)** *concealed in the pines of the Goathorn peninsula, in a view*
*north-eastwards to Sandbanks and Shell Bay* **(central background)** *in 1995.*

replace the wartime landing-craft. The most impressive were recycled warships, some of them only a few years old, such as motor torpedo boats with weapon-tubes in their bows. Hession looked back on his Goathorn days as the best in his life:

*I was the first to use the phrase about it turning into the millionaire's playground. Mine is the best location going. Both the smaller and bigger ships have grown in numbers each year and you can now fill the I-Spy book of boats in a single day. I keep them from landing if they look the sort to have guns. I will not have anyone killing animals or disturbing the birds. The children are self-taught, on textbooks and appropriate classics, such as Dean Swift's* Gulliver's Travels *which becomes real to us with Lilliput opposite and tales of smuggler Isaac Gulliver. They learn as much from the old-timers as from books. Tom Newman, the best boatbuilder in Poole, talks of his ancestors being the first shipbuilders for the Royal Navy, almost as if it was yesterday. Listening to*

*him, it is as if Henry VIII was our last significant ruler, in the way that the rest of us talk about Queen Victoria.*

Post-war cultivation covered much of Major Dudley Ryder's 5,123-acre Rempstone Estate with Forestry Commission conifers, mostly from 1948 to 1950, but the family retained the mineral rights. Traditionally, these were for ball-clay extraction, but to almost everyone's surprise an oil reservoir of immense proportions was discovered at Wytch Farm (SY 980 853) in 1973, after years of fruitless seismic surveys and exploration failures across the UK. Petroleum production licence PL 089, jointly held by the Gas Council and pre-privatisation British Petroleum, had hit the bull's-eye beside Poole Harbour.

In 1974, when more oil was being discovered in Purbeck than the whole of Texas, the targeted stratum was Bridport Sands lying up to 3,500 to 4,000 feet below the ground. These oil-impregnated sandstones of the Jurassic and Triassic ages are between 144 and

248 million years old and are the result of organic decay of liptinite, exinite, and vitrinite materials at temperatures between 95 to 105 degrees centigrade. Despite the strong sulphurous smell below the nodding-donkey beam pump that has been a coastal oddity at Kimmeridge Bay since 1959, the oils from this deposit are sulphur free and of the finest quality. Known as 'British light sulphur-free' they need minimal refining though they are mixed with heavier Arab oils for the manufacture of end products.

A larger, deeper – and for many years untapped – Sherwood reservoir was discovered in 1978. It is this that is reached from Goathorn peninsula. Oil analyst Lesley Brown drove me around Goathorn and some of the more scenic heathland nodding donkeys in 2000. She explained that though the Purbeck field still has about 60 active oil wells, mostly mechanical nodding donkeys, these beam pumps only lift a maximum of 2,000 barrels a day (a barrel is 35 gallons) from the Bridport reservoir 900 metres below, whereas an electronic pump is capable of bringing up 20,000 barrels from the deeper Sherwood reservoir, at 1,600 metres below Poole Bay. Of the remaining reserves, about 30 million barrels are in the Bridport strata, whereas the Sherwood has an estimated 370 million barrels. There is a considerable usage of sea water 'as a pressure support' to encourage the oil to rise from the wells. Some 85,000 gallons a day are extracted from Poole Harbour, by a plant on Cleavel Point, opposite Green Island. Leslie Brown put the operation into perspective:

*The flow has already peaked. It reached 101,000 barrels in 1998, dropping to 82,000 barrels in 1999,*

*and estimated at 78,000 gallons for 2000. It's become a mature field and is now in a gradual decline. We are still drilling but no longer exploring, with the additional effort going into pockets not yet reached, as in-filling to side-track off an existing well hole to a different part of the reserve.*

She described the demobilisation of the M-site on Goathorn peninsula in February 2000 as 'the end of an era'. It had been in operation since 1993 and even made an appearance on Admiralty charts, though with a 'mobile' tag. The Deutag T47 drilling rig was 60 metres high and had an extended reach of five kilometres, with half that distance being under Little Sea, Studland beach and the extremity of Poole Bay. Its demobilisation and dismantling was accompanied by the placing of tree trunks and other truck-calming measures to ensure that roadside verges were not damaged by departing leviathans.

BP pointed to the honouring of its 'Wytch Farm Promise' that the Purbeck landscape was on loan and would be returned untarnished as withdrawal took place. By 2025, on current estimates, it is quite possible that no one will know they have been, though someone is bound to mount a campaign to save the original nodding donkey on the Kimmeridge cliffs for the National Trust, along with the obsolete mobile-phone mast and representative pylon line, as technology moves on. The Warner family at Goathorn Farmhouse – at the time of writing Edward, Juliet, Nicholas, Rosemary and Sebastian – and re-introduced pine martins may soon have the peninsula to themselves.

# Chapter 6
# PIRATES & PLUNDER

*Smugglers landing kegs in a corner of the bay.*

**Below:** *A smuggler with pistols and sword.*

The most famous of Dorset pirates, born in 'La Pole' and said to lurk behind Old Harry Rocks to prey on vessels approaching his home port, left legends that lasted the millennium. The site of his birthplace was still being pointed out in the Old Town at Poole, on the corner of Carter's Lane and Hill Street between the High Street and Dear Hay Lane, long after it had been swept away by Georgian redevelopment. By 1402, Henry Pay or Harry Paye – rendered in Spanish as 'Arripay' – had been reported to the Privy Council for seizing vessels trading between Castile and England, contrary to a treaty between the two states. He was blamed in May 1403 for taking wine from the *Seint Anne*. Audaciously, he was also active in the English Channel, it being alleged in November 1403 that he had taken a ship at sea between Poole Bay and St Catherine's Point and brought it into Freshwater, Isle of Wight, to unload '3,500 quintals of iron and 100 costilles of avoirdupois'.

By February 1404, Diego Lopes de Astunyga complained of a similar loss, plus a mule and gilded items valued at '5,000 nobles of the King's money' in a resisted boarding which resulted in many being killed and others wounded. The vessel, from Bilbao, was seized and its surviving crew put in a boat and left to row themselves to France. Pay, once again, was seen heading for his refuge in the Isle of Wight. Later in 1404 he was accused of piracy against the *Seinte Marie*, also Spanish, with a mixed cargo valued at 12,000 gold nobles. This included hides, suet and wax as well as the usual imports of iron.

Poole was accused by Spaniards of harbouring a nest of pirates of which Harry Pay, in a wonderful phrase credited to the Count de Buelna, was 'a knight who scours the seas as a corsair with many ships'. To paraphrase his accusations, all Poole men were pirates, and the town's fishermen were women. In 1404, it suited the English authorities to have it this way, as Henry Pay was legitimised as a privateer, and made a commander of the Cinque Ports. The Welsh had declared independence from the English, with Owen Glendower declared Prince of Wales, and their revolt had been recognised by Charles V of France.

Having lost his vessel to capture by a Norman barge, Henry Pay shouted his 'war cry' at a critical moment. Shackled colleagues turned on the French, freeing themselves and slaughtering all of their captors, in both Pay's vessel and the barge. Instead of lowering the enemy flags they left them flying and headed for the Seine. Gathering a scratch English fleet they exacted swift revenge by plundering French vessels along the estuary.

Pay's activities became fully legitimised when he was commissioned to escort the King's daughter, and her dowry, for her marriage to the Duke of Bavaria. Poole, though suffering an attack from the Spanish in which Pay's brother was killed, otherwise benefited from the fortunes of war. Based in Poole Harbour and Studland Bay, Pay made regular raids along the coast of Brittany, bringing back a total of 120 captured vessels and their cargoes in 1407. He advised on the management of the English garrison at Calais in 1414 and died on 25 March 1419 at Faversham, Kent, where he was buried in the church of St Mary of Charity and commemorated with a fine brass memorial.

The next phase of Purbeck piracy coincided with the appointment of Queen Elizabeth's current favourite, Sir Christopher Hatton, as Lord Chamberlain, after which he bought Corfe Castle, its manor, and the Royal Warren of Purbeck. Hatton was more interested in his Northamptonshire properties and delegated his duties to Francis Hawley (died 1592). One of the ancient titles attached to governing Corfe Castle was Vice-Admiral of Purbeck, a kind of lord high admiral of local waters with plenipotentiary powers over visiting ships, including those of the Royal Navy.

Studland Bay and village thrived in a lawless vacuum – 'infested by pirates' – who brought captured

**Above:** *Poole pirate Henry Pay and his wreckers off Old Harry Rocks, painted by Harry Crow in 1992.*

**Background:** *Pirate commander Henry Pay in a detail from Harry Crow's painting.*

ships alongside the sandy beach for unloading. On-shore services included hostelries and a market. The Elizabethan equivalent of a car boot sale was a boat sale of privateer booty which attracted bargain hunters from across the county. They founded the hypermarket of the day, offering everything from silks, satins, damasks and mockadoes to fine clothes, rapiers, exotic fruits and wines. Bribes, allegedly, were paid to the Vice-Admiral and other officials.

Innkeepers and accommodation providers at Studland included Roger Munday and William Munday, who were brothers, and Mrs Chattock and Joan Penruddock. They were accused of running brothels for recuperating pirates. Admiralty intelligence described William Munday personally as 'the devil' and his house 'the hell of the world'. All types of goods and services were for sale and the prices most competitive.

Finally, the Privy Council reacted to travellers' tales from Dorset in 1572 and summoned Lord Thomas Bindon from Lulworth Castle and Sir Richard Rogers of Bryanston House to explain what was happening. Two warships were directed to intercept suspect vessels and the Dorset Commissioners gathered in special session at Corfe Castle. A haul of 17 pirates, including two named Callice and Piers, were tried and condemned. They were hanged in chains and lowered below the high-water mark at Studland. The Admiralty division of the High Court names Clinton Atkinson, Arnewood, Heynes, Purser, Vaughan and Walton as Studland pirates. Some may well have been aliases though Clinton Atkinson had a good pedigree. His godfather was none other than the Earl of Lincoln, Lord Admiral of England, as a result of which he won a pardon and returned to business at Studland.

In 1582 the people of Poole petitioned the Privy Council that the pirates infesting Studland Bay were molesting legitimate foreign shipping 'to the utter

# Smugglers

Above: 'Smugglers
Intrusion' from a
painting by Sir
David Wilkie.

Left: *Drinking on
the job.*

undoing of their trade'. John Piers and an associate named Walshe were convicted as a result and sentenced to be hanged, drawn and quartered. Their body parts were gibbeted around Purbeck.

Clinton Atkinson was captured again, in a sweep by HMS *Talbot* and HMS *Unicorn*, and hauled before Judge Julius Caesar in the High Court. When the news reached Corfe Castle, in 1584, John Uvedale – one of its two Members of Parliament – led a mob that stormed the castle in protest and is said to have done so much damage that Uvedale rebuilt his house from ashlars sent sliding down Castle Hill. Atkinson again tried to buy his way out of trouble, offering the then huge sum of £800, but this time he was sentenced to hang in chains at Wapping. Arnewood, however, was able to secure an acquittal but Studland also lost Heynes, Vaughan and Walton. Five other pirates were also convicted and executed.

The survivors included some of the nation's best seamen, as with

*Anti-smuggler, or Preventive Officer, as he was known.*

Henry Pay at the beginning of the previous century, and like him many later went to sea in answer to the nation's call, defeating the Spanish Armada in 1588. Others went on 'the long voyage' to explore and colonise the New World.

A threat regarded as legalised piracy stalked territorial waters during the French Wars of two centuries later. In 1794 the merchant vessel *Maria*, returning from Newfoundland to Poole, was ordered to 'Heave to' by a Royal Navy ship in Studland Bay. Ignoring this, Captain Randle continued north-westwards, on a direct course for the harbour entrance. The naval officers opened fire. Five persons were killed – the pilot, two members of the crew, and two passengers. Lieutenants Glover and Phillips of the Impress Service of His Majesty's Navy – better known as a press-gang – were charged with wilful murder. The judiciary granted bail, however, and allowed the matter to be adjourned '*sine die*'. Such a postponement is indefinite and effectively shelves a case for ever.

# Chapter 7

# PILOTS & FERRYMEN

Poole Harbour is a remarkable piece of landlocked water, five miles across but with an access only 350 yards wide, with double the normal tidal cycle in each 24-hour period. Inlets weave up and down contorted back channels and give it a total perimeter that stretches between 50 and 100 miles. Arguably, an apposite word as I receive letters on the subject, it is the second largest natural harbour in the world. Sydney is bigger and Freetown, in Sierra Leone, comes third.

The topography makes for long-term employment for pilots and ferrymen. The former ensure safe passage for visiting vessels and the latter enable us to cut a few of the corners. Incoming vessels are met by the Poole Pilot in Studland Bay. Some have lived in Studland Parish, notably William Hixon, a Poole pilot in Victorian times, whose home was Pilot's Cottage at Goathorn.

Ben Pond, boatman and 'wild man' of the 1920s, looked back half a century for me in 1970, and said he was sure that the historic ferry point from the South Haven peninsula was on the south-west side, on the harbour shore between Brand's Point and Jerry's Point. Here the silted site of Redhorn Quay (SZ 021 855) was served by Redhorn Lake and was far safer for boats than the Shell Bay extremity of the peninsula. It dated from a time when Sandbanks was inhospitable and users wanted ferries to go direct to Poole Quay. Ben Pond considered it was used, along with Ower Quay, for exports of Purbeck marble for the building of Salisbury Cathedral and imports of timber for the building of Corfe Castle:

*It is composed of huge square cut stone, tier upon tier, with deep water alongside. Fifty odd years ago there were deep wheel-ruts leading across the heath to Redhorn Quay. There were also the remains of stone bankers, like those at Swanage, where outgoing stone was stacked. Slowly the channel has been silting at its entrance from South Deep since about 1922. Mud becomes silt and the increasing harbour vegetation tends to cause more and more silt to find its way into the creeks and channels as rootage consolidates the higher mud banks.*

Ben Pond also pointed out that shoreline stones are not to be confused with the local geology:

*The first floating bridge on one of its earliest arrivals at Sandbanks in 1926, with a pedestrian ferry in the foreground and a yacht leaving the harbour, in a view south-eastwards towards Old Harry Rocks.*

*The transporter bridge at Middlesborough (note the ferry cage suspended from it) was the model for the crossing between Sandbanks and Shell Bay as proposed in 1904.*

*All have come from somewhere else, even the Purbeck ones from beyond Corfe Castle, and granite boulders used to turn up quite often. We would even see fresh ones! Many around Goathorn were granite with smart ones in Italian marble. It was a case of waterside dumping which still went on by ships that entered Poole Harbour to collect clay. The stone was ballast. In the old days, when they came for Purbeck marble and stone, they would either come with timber to sell or drop off other rocks into the mud.*

The present floating bridge between Studland and Shell Bay came about as a direct result of the failure of the Branksome Park and Swanage Light Railway project, proposed in 1904, which would have taken a tramway across a cage-and-chain suspension bridge from high steel towers on each side, comparable to the Middlesborough transporter bridge. Photographs of that make it look less than elegant. The *Bournemouth Graphic* reported:

*We are enabled to make public this week the official announcement that the plans and arrangements for an important development of the tramway system to Canford Cliffs and Swanage are practically complete. This is the first announcement that has been made on the matter, and we are in a position to give authentic details of the scheme in so far as present arrangements permit.*

*A private company has been formed, and among those taking a prominent part in its working, we believe, are Sir John Burt, of Swanage, and Mr Bankes, of Corfe Castle, to establish a system of trams, which will start from the Westbourne Arcade, and run through Seamoor Road and Branksome Park, across Canford Cliffs to Sandbanks. Here it is proposed to erect a tower on either side of the water, and by means of a cage and chain arrangement to swing the cars across to the opposite bank and thence continue the system to Swanage. We understand that it has not yet been decided whether the line of the route will pass through Studland, though the whole scheme is complete in all but one or two minor details.*

*The capital of the company is to be £68,000, and we are informed that practically the whole of the sum has already been privately subscribed. No appeal will therefore be made to the public.*

As the report said, this scheme was promoted by contractor Sir John Burt of Purbeck House, in Swanage, Walter Bankes of Corfe Castle and Kingston Lacy Estates, and Lord Wimborne representing the even more powerful Cornelia, Lady Wimborne, who was the aunt of Winston Churchill. Between them they owned everything of significance en route from Canford Cliffs and Sandbanks to Studland and Ulwell. Power for the tramway would have been provided by the Bournemouth Electricity Supply Company. The capital required for the project rose to £266,000 in 1906 as opposition mounted from Poole Harbour Commissioners and borough councillors in Poole.

Having blocked the proposal for the bridge, at a time when most of Sandbanks was sand dunes, the Harbour Commissioners recognised the need for an 'ambitious vehicle-carrying ferry service' between Poole and Purbeck in 1914. The timing was doomed. From 4 August, with the declaration of hostilities against Germany, the only pedestrian service from Sandbanks to Studland was by motor boat, which anchored offshore. William Payne, from Vine Cottage, lowered a dingy and rowed his passengers ashore. The Scott family of Sandbanks retained the monopoly for providing a ferry of long standing across the harbour run and were generally credited with having coined the delightfully descriptive Shell Bay name to lure visitors across to what the map still calls South Haven Point.

Post-war plans for a car ferry from Studland to Shell Bay were promoted by businessman Frank Aman of Totland Bay, Isle of Wight, who bought the Alum Chine Hotel in Bournemouth and had family expertise and financial support from sons Gerard, an engineer, and Arthur, a stockbroker. They enlisted pioneer motorist John Walter Edward Douglas-Scott-Montagu, 2nd Baron Montagu of Beaulieu (1866–1929), as first chairman of their Bournemouth–Swanage Motor Road and Ferry Company. Its incorporation was formalised by its own Act of Parliament in July 1923.

Bankes Estate land was to be provided from South Haven Point, southwards for three miles through Studland Parish, via a bog at Pipley Bridge, to the telephone box in Studland village. A road was to be laid on a strip 50 feet wide with a carriageway of 25 feet and verges of 12 feet 6 inches on either side. Users would be charged at a toll box beside Pipley Bridge.

It took three years before services began. Ferry No. 1, otherwise unnamed, built by J. Samuel White on the Isle of Wight, was steam-driven from coal boilers. Right from the start, on 15 July 1926, it proved popular and adaptations were soon carried out to increase its capacity, originally for 12 cars, to produce space for 15 vehicles. A total of 12,000 cars and 100,000 passengers were carried in the first curtailed season of only a couple of months.

The family name on site, at the introduction of the vehicle-carrying chain ferry in 1926, was that of the Harris brothers who were fishermen from Ower Quay. Linking them with latter-day ferries has been the memory or ghost of former skipper Roy, who is said to return as a phantom hand that turns lights on and off. Another aspect of continuity is that there is always a current Charlie, as the resident herring-gull is always called.

In 1929 the Ferry Company made its own application for a bridge but a private Bill was blocked in the House of Commons in 1930, due to a lack of local support. Plans show a circular ramp rising 120 feet to a suspension bridge with a central span of 600 feet between its towers.

The post-war ferry service from Studland to Shell Bay was in keeping with those austerity years. On returning to public use from military requisition, Ferry No. 1 frequently broke down, and was supplemented by Ferry No. 2. This could only carry eight cars and was borrowed from the River Medina, where it crossed from West Cowes to East Cowes on the Isle of Wight. Something more adequate was

*The business end of Ferry Road, looking southwards from the Shell Bay side of the water, with vehicles driving down the slope to board the floating bridge in 1935.*

again suggested and the third attempt at providing a bridge between Sandbanks and Shell Bay failed in 1955. By now environmental considerations were entering the frame and concern was expressed that any bridge would be obtrusive and unsightly.

Ferry No. 3, which came into service in 1958, was built by J. Bolson and Son Limited of Poole, makers of wartime landing-craft. With an overall length, including loading prows, of 157 feet, and a beam of 42 feet 6 inches, it had a loaded draught of 3 feet 6 inches. Power was provided by three Ruston diesel engines. These made for reliability, as it generally operated on two engines and could function on just one if necessary. Capacity was 28 cars and the annual total soon rose to some 650,000 vehicles, up to a 10-ton weight limit, with in excess of a million passengers.

Oil exploration was taking place in the Isle of Purbeck, with the first operational well being drilled at Kimmeridge in 1959, yielding 13,000 tons of crude each year, and more oil being discovered in Dorset than Texas in 1974. Petroleum production licence PL 089 lived up to its early promise with a much deeper reservoir, stretching east from Wytch Farm beneath Studland Parish and out to sea, which has been tapped from the Goathorn peninsula.

Also in 1974, floating the possibilities for alternative energy, the Central Electricity Generating Board tested the water with a scheme for a £250 million hydro-tidal power station at Sandbanks. This, according to Swanage reporter George Willey, 'will bring in its train a bridge across the ferry at Shell Bay.' He commented that 'the material benefit to the Isle of Purbeck of improved access by road – solving all problems at present on the Wareham–Swanage route – would be enormous.' The proposal to harness the 36,000,000 tons of water rushing through the 1,000-foot wide channel four times a day, at speeds of three to four knots, came from a Weymouth engineer. 'Pie in the sky,' said the clerk to Poole Harbour Commissioners.

Under the heading 'Underwater bus' the *Daily Mail* reported on Monday 3 March 1986 'why the 150 turned up a little late'. It 'got rather out of its depth trying to catch the ferry'. A pipe snapped and locked the brakes as the driver of service No. 150 went down the ramp on Saturday to catch the floating bridge from Shell Bay to Sandbanks:

*Before anyone could shout 'all change' the driver and his lone passenger abandoned bus and the ferry, operated by chains, was clanking to the rescue. Sliding in the front of its ramp under the red single-decker, the*

**The fourth ferry, Bramble Bush Bay,** *photographed midway across by Rodney Legg in a view southwards from Sandbanks to Shell Bay in 1999.*

Left: *Ferry No. 3 coming ashore at Shell Bay in 1983, photographed from the south-east by Colin Graham as a man and his poodle splash aboard.*

*The underwater bus of February 1986
in a view from the slipway at South Haven Point.*

*craft struggled mightily to keep the vehicle's roof above
water as the sea poured in. Soon, however, there was
no sign of the No. 150, so they sent for the Marines.
Yesterday frogmen plunged in, freed the brakes, and
the bus was towed clear, 18 hours late.*

The ferrying business would have taken on a new
dimension had Hook Island been built. Planned for
construction in Poole Bay, three-quarters of a mile
east of the harbour entrance (SZ 870 050), this 25-acre
artificial island was proposed by BP Exploration in
1990 to extract oil from an extension of their Wytch
Farm field. It would have surrounded and protected
an offshore oil rig. A private Hook Island Bill was
drafted for passage through the House of Commons
but was dropped after sustained opposition from
environmentalists and local authorities.

The Ferry Company's association with the Aman
family was weakened with the deaths of Frank and
Gerard Aman, before and after the Second World
War, and ended when second son Arthur Aman sold
his residual interest to Raglan Property Company in
1961. They submitted plans to landowner Ralph
Bankes that were regarded as irresistible. In this they
had not reckoned with a practising recluse who knew
his own mind. Back came the message, from his
agent, that 'Mr Bankes has no need to sell land at
Shell Bay and the last thing he wants is to see it
turned into another Sandbanks.' No, they were
firmly told, there was no point in meeting Mr Bankes.
The encounter convinced him that the right course
was to leave his land to the National Trust.

Raglan sold the Ferry Company to Silvermist
Properties (Chelmsford) Limited, a firm with shipping interests in South America, which was then
re-structured as a division of the Fairacres Group.
Managed by Rodney Kean and his family they
provided new slipways, offices and tollbooths, with
mechanised and centralised payments, and the
introduction of mains electricity to Shell Bay. That
used to be provided by generators and a windmill.
Concentration of toll collection at Shell Bay enabled
closure of the toll box 'in a hut beside the mosquito-
infested swamp' at Pipley Bridge.

Seafarer Nick Gosney, master of the floating bridge
named *Bramble Bush Bay*, is the third generation of
the family to captain the Bournemouth–Swanage
Ferry. It takes just three minutes to link the 350 yards
of missing road between the former North Haven
Point and South Haven Point, which are now univer-
sally known as Sandbanks and Shell Bay (with the
actual Bramble Bush Bay being around the corner in
Poole Harbour).

The fourth ferry between Studland and Shell
Bay, *Bramble Bush Bay* was built by Richard
Dunston Limited at Hessle on the Humber, and is
244 feet in length with a beam of 54 feet. Her
loaded draught is 3 feet 9 inches. She came into
service in January 1994 and her capacity is 52 cars
at a time. The fiscal year total for 1999–2000
reached 786,909 cars, in addition to 9,418 buses and
coaches, 3,803 trucks, 66,396 bikes and motorcycles,
and 194,373 pedestrians. That amounts to three
million people.

**Bramble Bush Bay** *fully loaded at Shell Bay in 2000, in a view south to the Purbeck Hills.*

Two 9-ton chains of hardened steel hold the vessel on its course across a lively piece of water, as the engines ride this underwater wire between two concrete slipways. Each chain is 1,235 feet in length and only one is operational at a time. They last about 15 to 18 months, stretching as they wear, with a couple of links being removed each fortnight to maintain constant length and tension. The powered side of the floating bridge is always that away from the flow of the tide (harbour-side on incoming tides and sea-side on outgoing tides). Much of the wear is caused by the concrete slipways. Lengths of old chain are used locally for moorings and anchoring the nets in Scottish salmon farms. 'They are excellent for that,' says Nick Gosney, who has been manager of the Ferry Company since 1986.

Either side of the crossing there are sandy peninsulas with the best sandy beaches in England. Cross-channel ferries the size of multi-storey car parks come and go, as do the biggest collection of yachts in northern Europe. There is still occasional talk of reviving the project for a bridge.

The transition of the northern end of its proposed site into the most expensive real estate in Europe has since made any starting point a practical impossibility. On the other side of the water, the bequest by Ralph Bankes of all his lands to the National Trust, on his death in 1981, has deprived the scheme of a destination. In between there is another problem. The maximum height of vessels operating from Poole Quay and Hamworthy reached the sky with Brittany Ferries. For example *Barfluer*, at the top of its radar antennae, is 139 feet from the Plimsoll line. Car-less she rises even further out of the water. Any bridge would have to provide at least 200 feet clearance above high tide.

None of these realities will stop people suggesting a bridge, particularly after having waited in queues on each side of the harbour, but that congestion is another reason why it will never happen. 'Speeding the cars across the water will bring total gridlock,' ferryman Nick Gosney explained. 'It's only because we control the numbers that people still have somewhere to go.'

Some have encountered problems while trying to head in the opposite direction. 'A Flippin' Hero!' was how the *Sun* newspaper headed one of the best silly-season stories of August 2002. 'Georges the dolphin halts ferry so cops can nick gems gang.' Three young men were driving north from Swanage, allegedly, after a jewellery shop had been raided. 'Coincidence or not, Georges saved the day,' said the wonderfully named Inspector Nick Mason (though he may not be). The 8-feet-long dolphin was swimming with children from Sandbanks. As a result the ferry service was temporarily suspended. 'It was about to leave with our suspects aboard when Georges arrived on the scene,' Inspector Mason explained. 'The operators were worried about sailing over him and delayed the departure.' The police car in not-quite hot pursuit was therefore able to catch up with the likely villains. Arrests were made but no stolen rings were recovered: 'We believe they were thrown overboard.' Perhaps Georges could find them.

*Bridge watch from* **Bramble Bush Bay** *in 2000, looking out for yachtsmen pushing their luck.*

## Chapter 8

# SHIPWRECKS & SALVAGE

Maud Mary *was the last sailing ship in distress off Old Harry Rocks, in 1939, providing a picture that typifies shipwrecks through the ages.*

The Runciman Committee on Historic Wrecks listed a Studland wreck of about 1480 as 'the sixth oldest so far discovered in British coastal waters' and the one with 'the most substantial surviving timbers'. This 'wreck of great historical significance' was given top priority after January 1984 when two divers from Hamworthy Sub-Aqua Club disentangled a snarled trawl net. They found it wrapped around rib timbers which were planked for a length of 85 feet. There was also what appeared to be a gun barrel.

Quantities of broken pottery streamed from splits in the hull. The pieces appeared at first to be black but on cleaning were found to be decorated with blue bands and 'strange Gothic lettering'. Martin Dean arrived from the National Maritime Museum and London experts soon identified distinctive Spanish ceramics of the type known as Isabella polychrome.

The pottery is so rare in Britain that 79 fragments retrieved from Studland Bay soon represented the 'largest collection of its type in England today'. The tin-glazed blue and purple ware from Seville is more often found in the West Indies than Europe, and seems to have been used by the Spanish themselves, rather than being manufactured for trade.

A total of about 40 receptacles from the wreck were probably in daily use on the vessel, rather than being cargo, and there were also several examples of Colombian plain pottery and copper lustre ware. The latter, from Valencia, was traded in small quantities but is also rare in England. A few sherds were also found of Saintonge vessels from south-west France. A total of 350 other finds included pieces of rope, string, cloth, leather, barrel hoops, seeds, bone and iron objects.

75

Studland Bay Wreck Trust was formed as a joint venture between the Sub-Aqua Club, Poole Maritime Trust, and Poole Borough Council. 'Much more lies beneath the sands,' they concluded after American marine surveyors Klein Associates searched the site with sonar equipment, and the wreck was confirmed as 'a lightly constructed caravel that represents a 500-year-old time capsule from a transitional period when ship design was in a state of flux.'

The wrought iron 6-inch breech-loaded gun barrel was raised from the wreck on 21 August 1989 and initially stored in Poole. On being taken to the Royal Armouries in the Tower of London, on 5 October 1989, it was given the accolade of 'Britain's oldest firmly dated cannon'. Two breech blocks were also recovered as well as five stone cannon balls. The vessel also carried anti-personnel guns of two or three inches diameter bore. The base and valve of a pump is one of only three known from these times. The others are from the *Mary Rose* off Spithead and *San Juan* which foundered off Newfoundland in 1565.

The discovery by a walker of a boomerang-shaped section of oak stern-post, apparently from a substantial Tudor ship, raised hopes in 2001 that there was indeed another *Mary Rose* buried in the deep sands off Studland beach. Seven feet in length, it was washed ashore during a gale and found to be free of barnacles and other sea life, which implies that it had been preserved in offshore silt. Nancy Grace, the curator of the National Trust's local archaeological collection, reported:

*Much of the shape of the sternpost has been achieved by natural branch, which would indicate that the tree may have been trained especially into the profile and shape required for the ship. This was common procedure in the 1500s for shipbuilding, and the construction has been achieved using wooden pegs or iron nails, all of which are intact in the piece recovered.*

There may be other timbers preserved in situ. The coastline from Redend Point to Shell Bay has been gradually accumulating over the past four centuries which raises hopes for suitable conditions having existed for the preservation of a major wreck.

Dendrochronological study showed the timber rings were too wide apart for an accurate reading but the report shows that the tree came from a well-watered north-western European location. Prolific growth of knots confirmed it was from a parkland or hedgerow setting – allowing a spreading specimen – rather than a tree growing in dense forest where it would have to compete for moisture and light. The Nautical Archaeological Society concluded that this evidence for English oak rules out linkage with the medieval Spanish wreck which produced the fine pottery.

By 1466, the port of Poole was already attracting foreign vessels, with 59 being listed, compared with 34 from the Channel Isles and 31 from home waters. Imports and exports were worth £4,131. The distant trade was growing fast and in 1505 the foreign ships numbered 175, with the Guernsey and Jersey vessels dropping to 27, and 119 'native' ships. Two-way trade had reached £13,600.

**Lord John Russell,** *named for the nineteenth-century Prime Minister, washed ashore on South Beach while trying to go round Old Harry Rocks.*

**Opposite page:** *Contemporary prints of Armada period vessels.*

the fires and removed most of the treasure.

There had been an accident, Sidonia later admitted, but the rumour was that this had been deliberate sabotage. A non-Spanish gunner, a German or a Flem, had been whipped. In retaliation he had fired a gun and thrown the smoking weapon into a barrel of gunpowder as he jumped overboard. Either way, this was an own-goal.

The following morning the smouldering hulk of the *San Salvador* was abandoned by the Spanish. Sidonia ordered her sinking but the demolition party failed to remove all of the casualties. Many of them had appalling wounds. It became clear that the English were soon going to arrive. The Spanish had to leave their crippled vessel and her pathetic wounded.

Lord Thomas Howard inspected the wreck but his boarding party had no stomach for her: 'The stink in the ship was so unsavoury and the sight within so ugly.'

Captain Thomas Flemyng later approached in the *Golden Hind* and towed the *San Salvador* to Weymouth. The inventory of her fittings came to £846.5s.8d. including an empty treasure chest which is now in Weymouth Museum. The 'meticulous valuation' included 5,460 gallons of wine.

In November 1588 it was decided to take the *San Salvador* up-Channel, under sail, to Weymouth. She had been partially repaired but was barely seaworthy for the short inshore excursion. Her sails needed complete renewal, and the Governor of Portland Castle had offered replacement canvas, but it was thought that the existing rigging was in good enough condition for the 50-mile voyage. In fact the vessel was not up to half that distance and as she came round Durlston Head into Poole Bay she was taking in water. The English crew, numbering about 100, may have tried to beach her on

Even so, boats from Biscay and beyond were a rarity, with most coming from Cherbourg, Guernsey, Lyme Regis, Weymouth, Barfleur and St Malo. The next great expansion in Poole trade followed in the wake of the *Mathew* from Bristol, in which John Cabot reached Newfoundland in 1498 and explored the North American coast south to the 38th parallel. Fortifications followed to protect the landward end of the new trade routes with blockhouses being established at Branksea Castle on Brownsea Island and Studland Castle beside Old Harry Rocks.

The earliest known war relic in Studland Bay is the wreck of the Spanish carrack *San Salvador*. A three-masted armed trading vessel, sailing with the Armada, she was captured by the English in Lyme Bay and taken as a prize into Weymouth. It was decided to take her further along the coast, to the Royal Navy base at Portsmouth, but on coming round Durlston Head she encountered difficulties. The vessel was brought into the sheltered waters of Studland Bay but sank. Numerous attempts have been made to locate the wreck, instigated by diver Roy Parker from Wimborne, but most of her remains have been swallowed by the shifting sands.

*San Salvador* was Miguel de Oquendo's vice-flagship and of importance not only to his squadron but the whole Spanish Armada because she carried the Paymaster-General and most of his gold. On Sunday 21 July 1588, after initial skirmishes off Plymouth, the *San Salvador* exploded. She was blown apart, losing her stern and killing 200 crew, as fire raged on the poop and top two rear decks. The Duke of Medina Sidonia brought his own vessel alongside to deal with

Imprinted at London by E. Allde for Hew Astley. 1592.

the sands of Studland Bay but she proved impossible to manoeuvre and went down off Old Harry Rocks. There, from 50 feet of water in 1984, diver Roy Parker brought up timbers that had come from a Spanish vessel. The *Lyon* from Studland rescued 33 of the crew but the remainder drowned.

In July 1802, the sailing boat *Betsey*, heading up the English Channel towards Arundel, Sussex, foundered in Studland Bay with the loss of her captain and two crewmen.

The battered hulk of the American frigate USS *Chesapeake* was brought into Studland Bay and anchored as a war trophy in the summer of 1813. She had been captured by HMS *Shannon*, commanded by Captain Philip Bowes Vere Broke (1776–1841) who was severely wounded in the action, off Boston on 1 June 1813.

Among the unknown losses in Studland Bay were three schooners, dashed to pieces on the shore in a hurricane on 11 February 1866. Phenomenal easterly winds pushed the sea to the top of the beach. 'Judging from the size of the vessels 17 or 18 persons must have been lost in them,' it was reported. A further 11 ships were also lost in the vicinity, and the village skyline was transformed, with the levelling of 99 great elms. It was noted by Victorian villagers that the rooks did not return to Studland until the turn of the twentieth century.

The seamen had been lost without trace, with a single exception, whose body was washed up on Studland beach. An anonymous donor presented St Nicholas Parish Church with a new set of communion plates in commemoration of the storm.

In the early hours of 17 January 1879 the USS *Constitution* nearly came to grief on shingle near Old Harry Rocks. The boom of her guns announced her predicament as the three-masted vessel languished at broadsides to the chalk cliffs. The United States frigate was carrying products from France, bound for the Paris Exhibition on the other side of the Atlantic, and found herself out of control in easterly winds as she came down the Channel.

Morning light enabled boats from Swanage and Poole to come alongside and remove guns, chains, cable and everything easily removable in order to lighten the vessel. Five steamers spent several hours in futile efforts to drag her clear. The rescue eventually owed its success to the additional pulling power of a Government tug which arrived in the afternoon from Southampton. *Constitution* was towed to Portsmouth for examination in dry dock, where only minor damage was found.

Exactly a week later, on 24 January 1879, the 500-ton Norwegian timber schooner *Annie Margretta* ran into the Handfast Point headland only a few hundred yards from where the *Constitution* had been stranded. It too was en route from France to the United States. By the afternoon, however, she was a total wreck. Swanage Lifeboat had difficulty getting down its slipway on Peveril Point, against heavy waves driven sideways into Swanage Bay by a continuing easterly wind. These difficulties persuaded the Lifeboat Institution to build a groyne to hold back the sea. As for the more immediate problem, the Studland wreck below Ballard Head, it was auctioned for £45.

In 1889, while heading up-Channel from Jersey to Southampton, the schooner *William Maskill* became a total loss on the ledge beside Old Harry Rocks. The crew of four were rescued by the Swanage Lifeboat, *Charlotte Mary*, and landed on Studland beach. Her cargo was coal tar and barrels of grease.

Studland was touched by the most famous shipwreck of all time when the *Titanic* collided with an iceberg on its maiden voyage in 1912. By 18 April 1912 the bad news in the *Dorset County Chronicle*, amplified in the *Bridgwater Mercury* on 20 April, was that 'a Studland gardener named Gibbons was working his way out as a steward.' He was listed as missing 'and leaves behind a wife and four [five, actually] children.' Jacob William Gibbons, born in 1875, lived at Harbour View and was the head gardener to the Honourable Eustace Fiennes MP who lived in the cliff-top residence known as Studland Bay. 'He went to sea to improve his health, to recover from peritonitis which weakened him for gardening,' Mrs Lottie Jane Gibbons told reporters.

In the event it seems to have done no harm at all, as he was saved in Lifeboat Number 11, and lived until 25 February 1965. He died in Swanage Cottage Hospital and his ashes lie beside Studland Methodist Chapel. Charles Burgess from Swanage was another Purbeck survivor.

*The curious thing was that the 'berg had been seen by passengers early in the morning and they mistook it for cloud,' Jacob Gibbons said, in one of the classic accounts of the disaster. 'I had just gone below and turned into the 'glory hole' – as our sleeping quarters are termed – and was hanging up my watch when I felt a sudden jolt. The shock was quick and slight and to this fact I attribute the great loss of life. Many of those aboard must have gone to sleep again under the impression that nothing serious had happened.*

*Memorial to Titanic survivor Jacob Gibbons.*

*Some went back for their nick-knacks and one lady, already covered in furs, complained that she had left more behind. She had a lucky mascot, in the shape of a pig, which played a tune, and refused to leave the ship until she had secured her treasure.*

On deck, however, he found a general reluctance to abandon ship:

*The boats were being lowers away but many passengers seemed to prefer sticking to the ship. Having helped some passengers, including two little children, into boat number 11, I scanned the deck for others but could see nobody about. Mr Wheat, another steward, was in charge and we drew away from the ship to a safe distance, about half a mile. Then we saw her sink. The cries of those on board were terrible and I doubt if the memory of them will ever leave me. They say it was denied by many that the band was still playing, but it was doing so. The strains of 'Nearer My God to Thee' came over the water with a solemnity so awful that words cannot express it.*

Mrs Gibbons, the former Miss Lottie Hammett, was related to two of the Tolpuddle Martyrs and is buried there, at Tolpuddle Methodist Chapel. By 1912, Jacob and Lottie Gibbons had five children – Edith, Annie, Freda, William and Lottie – with Arthur being born in 1916. Jacob Gibbons went on to travel North America as an employee of the Canadian Pacific Railway. In the First World War, to give thanks for his salvation, he returned to Europe with the Red Cross and served at the Battle of Verdun. Back in Studland, Jacob Gibbons was the accomplished chef in his wife's guest house at Harbour View which offered 'apartments; home comforts; board if required'. In retirement he became the vice-president of South Dorset Liberal Association. Newcomers to Studland were treated to a basket of his fresh vegetables which appeared overnight on their doorstep as a welcome to the village.

Sailing accidents became commonplace in Studland Bay during the twentieth century. Off Ballard Head, midway between Swanage and

*Tragic gravestone to three young members of the Marten family who were killed in a yachting mishap on 30 July 1927.*

Studland, two pleasure craft were involved in a mishap with a paddle-steamer shortly before the First World War. PS *Stirling Castle* had pulled away from Swanage Pier, in reverse, and turned off Ballard Point to gather speed for Bournemouth. Vyvyan Floyd, who was out in a sailing boat, recalled the moment for me:

*After the steamer appeared from behind the cliff, its wake caught us, and we were swamped with spray. Suddenly, as we swayed about, the air was rent with a frightful din. Another small boat, only 100 yards from us, had been sliced in half. Four of its occupants, including a mother and her two children, were drowned.*

That afternoon the father, from Australia, arrived at Swanage by train and was met at the station by the vicar. The Australian was carrying a doll for his young daughter who had been taken out in the boat for her birthday treat. The doll was buried with the little girl at Studland. Mrs Floyd, who remembered the day so vividly, never sailed again. To her, the most traumatic thing in the whole affair was that the body of the mother was later washed up on Swanage beach, immediately below the house where the grieving father was staying.

Mr Ben Pond, a boatman in Poole Harbour, told me this was not the only accident involving the *Stirling Castle*. Though only on the Bournemouth, Swanage and Poole run for two seasons, in 1913 and until the outbreak of war in 1914, she soon established a reputation for record speeds:

*We reckoned she was the fastest paddle-steamer we had seen. She could pick up speed in no time and definitely sank at least two other yachts. Her size was impressive too, with a length of 175 feet and beam 24 feet, but her career was cut short by the war. She returned to Southampton in October 1914. We missed her predecessor, Lord Elgin, which had given distinguished service since being introduced by the Bournemouth Steam Packet Company, way back in May 1881. Lord Elgin continued without a break for three decades, until the autumn of 1912, and to us was always a familiar and reassuring sight.*

An elaborate gravestone at Studland records a tragedy between the Milkmaid Bank and the entrance into Poole Harbour, in which three young members of the Marten family drowned: 'The two elder children gave their lives in a gallant attempt to save their younger brother and sister.'

They were the children of Major and Mrs A.J. Marten of Woodhay, near Newbury, who were on holiday at a bungalow named Sulva in Swanage. They took out a 15-foot sailing dinghy from the jetty at Studland on the morning of 30 July 1927. Moving northwards, close inshore, they found themselves trapped in choppy water in the north-west corner of Studland Bay before the Training Bank was built to form the eastern extremity of Shell Bay. The keel dragged in the sand as the south-westerly wind tipped the sail seawards. No one noticed them capsize.

Angela Marten (aged 21), debutante and accomplished swimmer, attempted reaching the nearby beach but disappeared into the waves. Midshipman Lawrence Marten (17), a cadet who was about to join HMS *Victory* in Portsmouth Harbour, stayed with the boat to look after the younger children as they clung to the side. They shouted and waved to motor boats coming and going from the harbour but no one spotted them. An hour later Henry Willoughby Marten (11) weakened and lost his grip, with the result that he drowned, and Lawrence as well in the attempt at hauling him back to the boat. Daphne Marten (14) continued hanging on for a further half hour and was then rescued by an observant party of Poole Sea Scouts, outward bound in their cutter *Mansel-Pleydell* for the Hamble estuary in Southampton Water.

They took Daphne to the ferry slipway at Shell Bay, still known as South Haven Point, from where she was driven to Swanage with news of the tragedy. Tilney Barton, passing in his yacht, attached a line to the dingy and brought it ashore.

Inset: *Ben Pond, photographed by Rodney Legg in 1971, recalled the 'good old days' of Lord Elgin, before 1912.*

USS Constitution *nearly became Studland's most famous wreck off Old Harry Rocks (excuse artistic licence) in 1879.*

# Chapter 9

# EMPIRE, SOLDIERS & WARS

A biographical headstone beside the porch of St Nicholas Church preserves the memory of Waterloo veteran Sergeant William Lawrence (1791–1869) who was the landlord of the Duke of Wellington pub, which is now the Bankes Arms. The old soldier had also gone through the South American and Peninsula campaigns with the 40th Regiment of Foot and won a gallantry award at Badajoz where he was wounded. Born at Briantspuddle, one of seven children, he was apprenticed at the age of 14 to Studland builder Henry Bush. Finding himself ill-treated and exploited he ran away with another boy to Wareham in 1806. Having moved on to Poole they had a close encounter with a naval press-gang and ran off as a blunderbuss was fired. It was with some relief that they were taken

into custody by a constable but they were less enthusiastic about being sent back to Swanage on the market boat. Terrified of returning to his master, William ran off across the heath, and hid in the fox earths beside the Agglestone.

Then he set off again for Wareham, spending the night in the Horse and Groom at Wareham, and went on to Dorchester. He was given food and a straw bed by an ostler on promising to enlist in the Army the following day:

*I was put into an old soldier's coat, and with three or four yards of ribbons hanging from my*

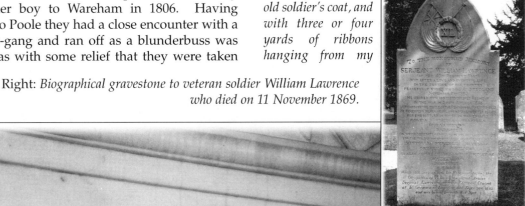

Right: *Biographical gravestone to veteran soldier William Lawrence who died on 11 November 1869.*

Above: *The memorial in Wimborne Minster to William George Hawtrey Bankes who was posthumously awarded the Victoria Cross in 1858.*

# Wartime Fun

*Historic photograph three times over.  Firstly for the divers, five-year-old Christopher Horn and his cousin, four-year-old Michael Walker.  Secondly for Studland Pier, seen in 1938, demolished as an anti-invasion measure in 1940.  Thirdly for the survival of this framed print, in the window of Joan and Helen Muspratt's photographic studio in April 1942 when it was hit by a German bomb. The photograph was salvaged from rubble lying in the street.*

*cap, paraded the town with other recruits, entering and treating someone or other in almost every public house.*

A neighbour from Briantspuddle recognised William and told his father. The family decided he was too young to go to war and told the recruiting officer that William was articled as an apprentice. A magistrate decided that he had to return to Studland. Once again William had other ideas, this time meeting a soldier in a public house at Winfrith Newburgh. He promised that if William could join him in Bridport he would make sure he was enlisted in the 40th Regiment of Foot.

Having passed through Dorchester at night, he caught the coach on the other side of the county town, at Winterbourne Abbas, to Bridport. The soldier took him to Taunton where he signed up and received a bounty of £2.2s.0d. Training took place at Winchester, Portsmouth and Bexhill, en route to Montevideo. Christmas 1807 was spent on the high seas off Cork, and the regiment then found itself under the command of Sir Arthur Wellesley, 1st Duke of Wellington, for the long slog across the Iberian peninsula. They fought at Talavera and fell back to Torres Vedras in the winter of 1810. The sieges of Ciudad and Rodrigo were the prelude to the great blockade of Badajoz and the 'forlorn hope' of a breach through its walls as Lawrence led a ladder party and fell wounded.

After a period in hospital, promoted to Corporal Lawrence, he fought at Vittoria and pushed the French back across the Pyrenees as Napoleon Bonaparte was overthrown and peace declared. The 40th Foot hoped to return home by ship from Bordeaux, but were diverted to Ireland, Jamaica and New Orleans, where the British were at war with the new United States in 1812. On sailing for home yet again they were once more cheated of their glimpse of 'perfidious Albion'. Blighty was represented by the white cliffs of the Isle of Wight and the green hill above Portsmouth as they were intercepted by a frigate off Spithead. Napoleon had escaped from Elba and the 40th Foot was to divert to Ostend.

After the famous victory at Waterloo on 18 June 1815, for which Wellesley was rewarded with the Wellington dukedom, the regiment moved on to Germain-en-Laye for the winter occupation of Paris. Here Sergeant William Lawrence met Marie Louise Claire (1801–53) who ran a stall selling tobacco, snuff, spirits and fruit. His colonel reluctantly agreed to their marriage but insisted that the new Mrs Lawrence dropped her Marie Louise given names as they were those of Napoleon's first wife. It was as Clotilde Lawrence that she accompanied William on the march to Cambrai and Calais. They were picked up by a coal barge from Newcastle and went on to Glasgow.

Here, late in 1817, Lawrence heard that his father was ill in Dorset and was granted a six-week furlough

to go home. They sailed from Leith to London and took the coach to Salisbury. William and Clotilde then walked to Blandford, some 20 miles, which took from before breakfast until it was dark again. The following day they completed the last eight miles over the hills to Briantspuddle and arrived during the Sunday church service in nearby Affpuddle:

*I suddenly saw the old lady who had got scent of the matter coming like a spread-eagle with the same old black bonnet and red cloak that she had when I left her. Then I proceeded on to the old man, who was quite infirm and hobbling along behind on two sticks. None of us spoke for a long time, but at last the old man gave utterance to 'My child, I did not expect to see you again.' It was indeed 16 long years since I had left them at Dorchester.*

Four gallons of ale were fetched from the nearest inn, from Puddletown in the next valley, and 'we made ourselves comfortable till ten o'clock, when we retired to rest in the same room that I slept in 18 years before.' They visited relatives, including brother George Lawrence in Corfe Mullen, and then went to Bristol in the hope of a ship sailing for Glasgow. There was none. William and Clotilde, faced with the alternative of walking all the way to Scotland, sold his watch for subsistence, and arrived with her suffering frostbite, and only a day's leave in hand. That epic trek, almost Russian in its length and nature, was achieved despite William's knee wound for which he was granted 2d. a day pension in 1818, of a total of 9d. a day approved by Chelsea Hospital.

They were at last free, apart from another bout of sustained walking, which saw William deciding that it was now safe to return to Studland – 'the place where I had been apprenticed' – and 'claimed that rightly as my parish'. Even so, after he had been working for a retired sea captain, the long arm of the Army stretched again, and he was recalled in 1820 to the Third Veteran Battalion at Plymouth for a year on secondment to the Coastguard Service in County Kerry.

So ended a military career of 17 years 7 months, with a final walk from Plymouth to Studland, where he 'took a little public house'. As a boy, William Masters Hardy worked for George Bankes during the rebuilding of the Manor House in 1848:

*During the midday meal the men and boys would go down to the old public house, then named the Duke of Wellington, to partake of their meals and the ale which Mr Bankes allowed each workmen and boy, one pint being given to a man and half a pint to each boy. The landlord at the time was a Waterloo veteran named Sergeant Lawrence, who had also fought in the Peninsula campaign, and finally retired with several medals and about ten clasps. Although one hour, the usual time, was allowed for dinner, yet sometimes it took an hour and a half to get through the meal, especially when the old soldier was in an anecdotal mood and related some of his thrilling and desperate adventures. Pride spread over the countenance of old Lawrence as he retailed his yarn and his beer. It was a triumph of exalted genius.*

Clotilde died on 26 September 1853 and William retired to a thatched cottage across the road, since demolished, which stood between the public house and the back path to the Manor House. Sergeant Lawrence renegotiated his pension, having it increased to a shilling day, but despite feeling 'rather unwell' he lived for another 16 years.

He was still a living legend but the popularity of the Duke of Wellington had plummeted during his afterlife in politics. The public house was given a neutral name, the New Inn, until being named for the village's landowning family and in particular a gallant young man who won the nation's highest honour. Sadly, he only told his story to one non-combatant, but that was to the world's first war correspondent, who had made his name in the Crimea.

A hero of a famous siege in the Indian Mutiny, Cornet William Bankes VC (1837–58) recalled his Dorset sailing days in Studland Bay as he lay dying, in Lucknow. His European memorial is in Wimborne Minster:

*Sacred to the memory of William George Hawtrey Bankes VC, Cornet 7th Hussars, the fifth son of the late Right Honourable George Bankes MP of Corfe Castle and Kingston Lacy, county of Dorset. He fell mortally wounded whilst charging a body of rebels near Lucknow, on the 17th of March, and died on the 6th of April, 1858, aged 21 years. This tablet is erected by his brother officers as a token of personal esteem.*

He was talking about yachting, and having 'many a jolly cruise' as he lay dying with legs and arms hacked to pieces. The Victoria Cross for valour would be awarded posthumously by Queen Victoria to his mother at Kingston Lacy House. Cornet William Bankes, a subaltern, was buried beside the ruined

cantonment church that stood near the camp of the 7th Hussars. As well as the memorial in Wimborne Minster he is also commemorated by a stained-glass window in St Nicholas Church at Studland.

The correspondent for *The Times*, William Howard Russell, told the world of his courage in repelling a rebel charge at the end of the British siege of their stronghold at Lucknow on 19 March 1858:

*A band of Ghazees, who issued out of an old mud fort and charged the guns and the party of the 7th Hussars covering them, had got the lad down and hacked at him in that cruel way until he was rescued by his comrades. It is perfectly astonishing, to witness his cheerfulness, and resignation. 'If I get out of this, Russell,' the fatally wounded young man said, 'they tell me I'll be able to go yachting, and that's all I care about. We'll have many a jolly cruise together.' He paused for a moment, 'If it please God'.*

*William Howard Russell, the war correspondent of* The Times, *who told of William Bankes's valour and bravery.*

Bankes was dying in the hospital of the 53rd Regiment in the Indian Imam Bara temple palace at Lucknow. Russell described his injuries as frightful: 'One leg lopped off above the knee, one arm cut off, the other nearly severed, the other arm cut through the bone, and several cuts on the body.'

Whilst lying there he heard that Sir Colin Campbell – Commander-in-Chief, India – had recommended him for the Victoria Cross. The Prince of Wales, later Edward VII, accompanied by Lord Curzon as Viceroy of India, placed a wreath beside the grave of William Bankes VC before reviewing a line of veterans on a nearby lawn. 'The sacredness of India haunts me like a passion,' Curzon declared. Anglo-Indians would never forgot or forgive the Mutiny and a flag flew day and night over the shell of the Residency in Lucknow, which was preserved as a ruin, until the very day that Lord Mountbatten relinquished the paramountcy of the Raj on 15 August 1947. Then, it was finally lowered and the flag-pole torn from its foundations.

Studland's Waterloo veteran died in 1869, on 11 November, though the day and month had yet to acquire their special significance for old soldiers.

## Anti-invasion

Right: *Middle Beach on the front line in one of the experiments with tracked vehicles.*

Left: *One of the few surviving pillbox machine-gun posts at Studland, beside Knoll Beach car park, photographed from the south in 2000.*

Below: *Dragon's Teeth tank-trap obstacles across the valley behind the beach huts at Middle Beach in a view northwards towards Shell Bay, photographed by Rodney Legg in 2002.*

## Anti-invasion

Left: *Studland Bay on fire, preparing a warm welcome for German invaders.*

Below: *Oil-slicks across the water off South Beach, in a view north-westwards to Redend Point, as* Project Fougasse *is set for ignition in December 1940.*

Being a parish of 543 adults in 1911, with more youngsters reaching fighting age by 4 August 1914, it was inevitable that many families in Studland would be touched by the conflict that turned into the 'Great War' and is now remembered as the First World War. The war memorial in the church records their sacrifice from both sides of the social scale. The son of the rector, Revd Frederick Swift Algeo, was among them.

Captain William Bensley Algeo of the 1st Battalion, the Dorsetshire Regiment, who held the Military Cross, was killed on 17 May 1916. 'Fearless, resolute, indefatigable, he was one of the finest of soldiers,' the family were told. He had resisted selection as Staff Captain to the Brigade Commander: 'He said he had been with the old men so long he felt he could not forsake them.' With another officer he ventured into No Man's Land near Hammerhead Sap, beside Thiepval Wood above the marshes of the Ancre Bouzincourt, 'in broad daylight to try and locate some German machine gun emplacements', and neither were ever seen again.

Captain John Fiennes from Kya-Lami, which was renamed Studland Bay House, lost his life with the 1st Battalion, the Gordon Highlanders. He was the son of Sir Eustace Edward Twisleton-Wykeham Fiennes, the Liberal MP from Banbury knighted in 1916. Lieutenant Alastair Macleod from Wardley was with the Royal Horse Artillery. Lieutenant Curden Theodore Thomasset of the 20th Battalion, County of London Regiment, died at Loos, France, on 25 September 1915. He was five days away from his 21st birthday.

Corporal Herbert Davis and Private William Marsh were with the 1st Battalion, the Wiltshire Regiment. Private Henry Churchill was with the 1st Battalion, South Staffordshire Regiment.

Private Edward Rendell of the 1st Battalion, the Dorsetshire Regiment, died of his wounds on 30 July 1916. Private George Savage lost his life with the 1st Battalion, the Hampshire Regiment. Meanwhile, in the Royal Navy, farmer's son Sydney Summers from Wadmore died on HMS *Good Hope* and Henry Tupper on HMS *Monmouth*.

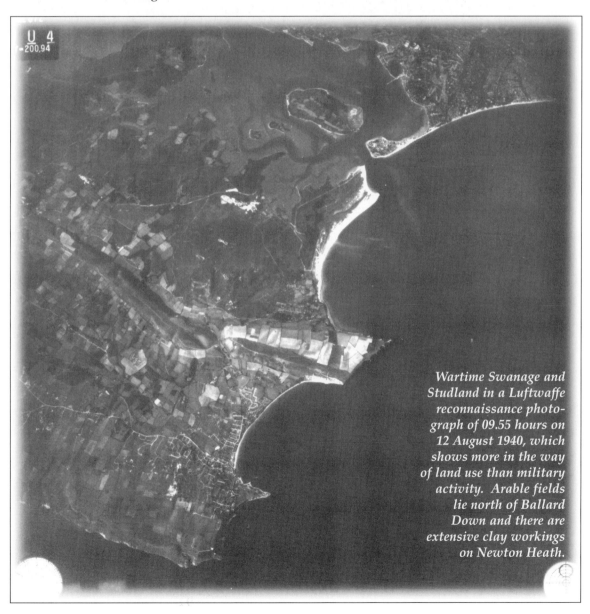

*Wartime Swanage and Studland in a Luftwaffe reconnaissance photograph of 09.55 hours on 12 August 1940, which shows more in the way of land use than military activity. Arable fields lie north of Ballard Down and there are extensive clay workings on Newton Heath.*

*The Heinkel bomber which crash-landed at Westfield Farm during the Battle of Britain.*

Nowhere in Britain was more at the sharp end at both extremes of the Second World War. Studland Pier was demolished in 1940 to prevent it being used by German invaders. British mines were laid under the sands, and concrete Dragon's Teeth anti-tank obstacles built across its inland approaches, watched from pillbox machine-gun posts and 4-inch coast defence batteries on Redend Point and Ballard Down. Seawards, however, mines laid by the Germans on the night of Saturday 8 June 1940 took their toll on shipping attempting to use the Swash Channel into Poole Harbour after the fall of France, despite clearances by Navy divers from Portland.

The Dutch boat *Princess Juliana* was blown up off the Training Bank on Wednesday 12 June. An heroic rescue was carried out by the appropriately-named Ivor Holland who was awarded the Order of the Red Lion by the Netherlands Government-in-exile. Three of the 15-strong flotilla bringing back remnants of the British and French Armies from St Valery-en-Caux successfully ran the gauntlet of the Swash Channel on Thursday 13 June. Then the fourth vessel, the *Abel Tasman*, exploded with the loss of all 11 of her crew from the Royal Navy Volunteer Reserve. Fortunately, she was otherwise returning empty. An order was flashed to the remainder of the fleet for them to turn around and head for Southampton instead.

These were the new C-type of magnetic mine which were triggered by the approach of a steel ship. British explosives experts were desperate to retrieve one intact for examination. Acting under Navy orders on Saturday 15 June, Poole fisherman Harold Cartwright in *Smiling Through* attached a 700-feet line to one near the Bar Buoy, and towed it into sandy shallows off Studland beach. It exploded, however, though 'without delivering more than a shock and a shake' to Cartwright and the boat.

The Germans were slow in deploying this potentially devastating weapon. The first to be dismantled

by the British was recovered at Shoeburyness, Essex, on 22 November 1940; the Germans had been lax in failing to incorporate an anti-handling device.

By Monday 1 July 1940, everyone on the Dorset coast was living in a Military Control Area, and were being issued with National Registration Identity Cards. Those for Sandbanks and Studland were issued by the Officer Commanding Troops, Poole Defence Area. Each carried a photograph and details of age, hair colour, height, build, distinguishing marks, occupation and nationality. To quote *Wartime Dorset*:

*Persons without cards who have business or private reasons for entering Military Control Areas will be required to give their names and addresses, and those of the people they are visiting, at police or military vehicle check-points. Passengers and pedestrians are also asked to co-operate. Police will be carrying out spot-checks inside these zones, and such as on buses, and at random in public places.*

Studland was also on the front line for the air war with numerous dogfights taking place overhead and crashes from both sides occurring on land within sight of the village or as an explosive splash offshore. Two forced landings, one from each side, were particularly noteworthy.

The beach, then a minefield, provided just enough emergency landing space for Flying Officer Alexander Rothwell Edge (1908–85) and Spitfire R6636 of 609 Squadron from RAF Warmwell after combat on Thursday 18 July 1940. Though covered by the sea it would be salvaged and fly again. The same applied to the pilot who was rescued unhurt by a Royal Navy launch. His fighting war was almost behind him, being posted the next month to Training Command, and promoted to Squadron Leader.

The devastating raid on the Bristol Aeroplane

Company's works at Filton on Wednesday 25 September 1940 – the single most successful enemy attack on an aviation factory during the Battle of Britain – was at some cost to the Luftwaffe. Five aircraft were lost, two returned with severe damage, and several needed minor repairs. Homeward-bound they were harried over Bath and the Somerset countryside by Spitfires of 152 Squadron from RAF Warmwell and Hurricanes of 238 Squadron from RAF Middle Wallop.

Flying Heinkel He.111 bomber G1+BH, with the markings to the left of the black cross on the fuselage identifying Kampfgeshwader 55, was Feldwebel Fritz Jurges (born 30 March 1915). He carried as observer and Kommandant [commander] his Staffelkapitan [squadron leader] Hauptmann Karl Kothke (born 9 September 1906). Bordfunker [wireless operator] was Gefreiter Rudolf Weisbach (born 7 December 1919). Bordmechaniker [flight mechanic and rear gunner] was Unteroffizier Josef Altrichter (born 10 November 1918). Bordschutze [gunner] was Flieger Otto Muller (born 12 May 1922). They were flying on one engine after being intercepted over Bath. Having almost passed over Poole, another crippled Heinkel He.111 (G1+LR) crashed at 12.09 hours and ploughed into Underwood, Westminster Road, Branksome Park. All but one of its five crewmen were killed. Within sight and sound of their demise, at 12.10 hours, G1+BH, also failed to begin its return across the English Channel to the safety of German-occupied France.

G1+BH and most of its occupants were luckier. Fritz Jurges realised they had no chance of reaching their air-sea rescue vessels in mid-Channel, let alone flying a further 75 miles to the Cherbourg peninsula. Turning westwards from Studland Bay, into a light wind, he achieved an almost immaculate forced landing on the edge of the heath on William Marshallsay's smallholding at Westfield Farm, Studland. Kenneth Wakefield, whose *Luftwaffe Encore* was published in 1979, interviewed surviving members of the crew and those living in Studland at the time who captured the aircraft intact and took the survivors prisoner. Karl Kothke recalled that they had been losing height rapidly:

*As bad luck would have it we passed over an airfield from which we could see fighters taking off, leaving clouds of dust behind them, and we knew the end must come soon. We tried in the end to dive for cloud cover, but the clouds were insufficient for our purpose, and at a height of about 6,000 feet we were again attacked by fighters. With our few machine-guns we stood no chance. Josef Altrichter, our flight mechanic, was badly wounded in his right leg and as he wore flying overalls we were unable to apply a tourniquet. We knew we could not help him.*

*We were then hit in our port engine which stopped as we crossed the English coast. All hopes of reaching mid-Channel now disappeared. We turned in over the*

*coast at a height of about 1,000 feet to attempt a landing and although the fighters were still following us they did not shoot any more. They knew we could not escape. We lost height very quickly now, heading straight for a quarry, but at the very last moment we managed to gain a little height and found ourselves over fields heading towards a small wood. We touched down and after sliding a short distance came to a standstill, a tree stopped up short.*

The crash in a mangold field was claimed by Pilot Officer John Spencer Wigglesworth of 238 Squadron. He circled above, watching as the Heinkel 'skidded on its belly', and almost severed a wing against a pole carrying power cables. Wigglesworth left the scene to refuel at Warmwell Aerodrome, near Moreton, and return to his base at Middle Wallop on the Hampshire Down. Born in Buckinghamshire, in 1920, he went on to the Far East and flew a Buffalo from Toungoo, Burma. He was killed on 6 February 1942 and is buried in Rangoon War Cemetery.

The village hero on the ground at Studland was Theo Janku, a Czech refugee who worked across the water as a wine waiter in a Bournemouth hotel, and spoke five European languages. Four Germans scrambled out of the machine:

*They were holding up their hands when I came up, 50 paces behind my wife, as I had stopped to pick up a Home Guard rifle. This, by the way, was not loaded. One of the Germans had hurt his spine and collapsed on to the ground. I told them to hand over their revolvers, which they did readily, but when I told them, again in German, to sit down and take it easy they stood dumfounded at hearing their own language in rural Britain and I had to order them again to do as they were told.*

*All relaxed then, except the pilot. Calling out to me that he had left a badly wounded man in the plane, he tried to get back to it. Covering him with my empty rifle I ordered him back – I would have no tricks with the plane and we would lift out his mate if there was one. About a dozen workmen came running down the hill, brandishing spades and picks which they then stopped when they saw that two Germans were hurt. They then did their best to make them comfortable.*

Mr and Mrs Marshallsay's bungalow provided facilities for tea-making. Mrs Ellen Marshallsay arrived, from Currendon Farm, with J.P.H. Warner of the Home Guard. A military medical officer did his best to save the wounded rear-gunner but he had a shattered thigh and died within half an hour. An RAF officer took command of the wrecked airframe and warned that there might be bombs on board. Then a detachment of the Suffolk Regiment, stationed in Studland, came with Colonel Keating and immediately pulled rank. 'Get the hell out of it,' one of the officers snapped at Studland villagers. 'This is a war, not a bloody peepshow.'

Colonel Keating had his Battalion Headquarters in Hill Close. The German crew were taken there and one member detained until after they had buried his dead comrade in Studland churchyard. He stood to attention and gave a Nazi salute as a colour party from the Suffolks fired a volley of shots over the grave.

For the surviving crew, as prisoners of war in Britain and then Canada, the conflict was over but their aircraft still had a role to play. It was recovered for examination by a civilian team from No. 50 Maintenance Unit, based in the Morris Motors works at Cowley, Oxford. They arrived with a transporter at the end of September. The bomber was under armed guard though the odd souvenir was removed, including a quarter of the swastika from the tail, on a detached panel of aluminium with two cannon holes through it.

For the recovery crew a drama turned into a tragedy when they snagged a wing in the overhead power cables beside which the Heinkel had come to rest. Two men were electrocuted and a third had serious burns. The airframe, however, went on to star in a charmed afterlife. After being searched for secret technology at the Royal Aircraft Establishment, Farnborough, it was reassembled for a War Weapons Week fund-raising appeal at Cathays Park in Cardiff. The vanquished Heinkel was exhibited beside a victorious Spitfire.

General Harold Alexander, General Officer Commanding-in-Chief of Southern Command, and Major-General Bernard Montgomery of 5th Corps, visited Studland on Friday 20 December 1940 and stood on the cliff top between Redend Point and Old Harry Rocks. They were promised the ultimate of anti-invasion precautions in which the sea was to be set on fire. Pipes had been laid from South Beach at Studland into the bay, as part of *Project Fougasse*, and a series of oil slicks were ignited. The surface of the sea was ignited and flared, with dense black smoke, until the waves began to disperse the slicks. Though as an anti-invasion measure it was only practical in favourable conditions the Germans would obviously try to choose an ideal day.

British intelligence suggested that German troops most feared being burnt alive in a conflagration on the beaches. It was therefore decided to authorise a deliberate breach of the blackout, by setting Studland Bay on fire at night, but this second attempt had to be abandoned due to a cold onshore wind which made the water choppy. The experiment was repeated, however, with dramatic results. It was said that you could read a newspaper in Bournemouth Square on the night of Sunday 2 February 1941.

A year later, Lieutenant Denys Wright from Studland lost his life, aboard HMS *Triumph*. The 1,090-ton submarine was reported missing on Thursday 5 February 1942.

The most evocative of Studland's war relics is a damaged photograph. It is a delightful study by professional photographers Joan and Helen Muspratt, featuring five-year-old Christopher Horn and four-year-old Michael Walker, as they jump into the sea from Studland Pier. The jetty became history in 1940, a casualty of anti-invasion precautions, and by April 1942 the photograph had been framed and

*High-speed splash by an amphibious armoured vehicle in a view south-eastwards to Old Harry Rocks.*

*The Churchill tank initially failed to climb Studland's dunes but then succeeded after a road of canvas and chestnut palings was laid by one of 'Hobart's Funnies'.*

was a pride exhibit in the Muspratt studio, gracing their Swanage shop window. Reporter George Willey told me what happened:

*The building was blown apart that month in one of the Luftwaffe hit-and-run raids that you have documented. The frame was smashed and the picture was found further along the street, in Institute Road, by someone who had the presence of mind to take it home and scribble a note on the back recording the event. Unfortunately the sisters' negatives were destroyed and most of their best work was lost. What makes the picture even more interesting is that Christopher Horn did well, and is now a Nottingham businessman, and Michael is back in Swanage as Wing Commander M. Walker, RAF retired.*

Lieutenant Maxwell Chevenix-Trench, from Studland, was killed in action in 1943 while serving with the Royal Engineers. His father, Brigadier Ralph Chevenix-Trench (1885–1974) had retired in 1941, as Signal Officer-in-Chief to Home Forces, to Little Westport in Wareham.

Giving a warm welcome to the Germans was no longer Studland's destiny as Hitler had unwisely decided to visit Russia instead. By the spring of 1944, however, the defences on Studland beach were being penetrated under live fire in the biggest rehearsals of assault landings ahead of D-Day. The big secret was where they would take place, with colossal spoofs being mounted to convince Hitler that they were destined for Calais and Greece rather than Studland's look-alike equivalent directly across the Channel on the sandy shores of Normandy. To protect participants from real-life Luftwaffe involvement, there was no publicity for Studland's contribution, or the fact that 80,000 men of the First United States Army were stationed in Dorset. The news blackout, under the respectable cloak of wartime censorship, extended to the arrival of King George VI at Swanage for dinner with the Generals on Monday 17 April 1944. They included General Sir Bernard Montgomery (effectively, for the assault, commander-in-chief of Allied land forces, also commanding the British 21st Army Group), General Omar Bradley (commanding the First United States Army), and Lieutenant-General Miles Dempsey (commanding the Second British Army).

The following morning 'Exercise Smash' hit the sands at Studland in a dramatic three-dimensional

*Amphibious vehicle moves up Middle Beach in 'Exercise Smash' on 18 April 1944, with landing ship US 526 offshore.*

## Exersise Smash

*Fort Henry, Studland's massive Observation Post built by Canadian Engineers in 1943, pictured by Rodney Legg from the front (top left),* back and inside *in 2002.*

**War Premier Winston Churchill, aka actor Graham Gadd, at the re-opening of Fort Henry by the National Trust on 18 April 2002.**

# Exercise Smash

**The Studland assault landing re-enactment of 2002, in a series of photographs by Rodney Legg.**

Right: *The approach to Middle Beach of a platoon of the American 'Fighting Firsts'.*

Above: *Below the café.*

Right: *Looking southwards with Fort Henry behind, on Redend Point.*

Below and inset: *The view across Middle Beach, south-eastwards, to Old Harry Rocks.*

## *Exercise Smash*

Above: *After a look-alike general Eisenhower composed the official picture, a crow swoops in the foreground.*

Left: *GIs fan out along the sand.*

*Advancing across the sand.*

# *Exercise Smash*

Left: *Protecting the withdrawal.*

Below: *Ascending the slope.*

*Headquarters car with spit and polish mirroring tents of the 1st Infantry Division of the United States Army, and photographer Rodney Legg posing as an officer, in 2002.*

battering from sea, land and air. As with the real D-Day, 'D' was the day and 'H' the hour with H-30 (H minus 30 minutes) being the approach time, governed by the tide, when landing-craft would come through 'the swept channel' offshore.

For the King, in the comfort of the now demolished Hotel Grosvenor, wake-up time was 04.00 hours. Police cars rang their bells and raced round each Purbeck village at dawn to tell residents to 'fully open all your windows'. This would reduce the risk of blast damage as Studland and Old Harry began to rock to the concussive thud of war. Taking part were elements of the United States 1st Infantry Division. 'The big Red One, otherwise known as the Fighting Firsts,' I said to their cheers as modern namesakes from Bournemouth carried out a small-scale re-enactment.

Andrew Purkis has a framed photograph in the lounge of Manor House Hotel at Studland, showing the scene on the beach as landing-craft and their vehicles rolled ashore. He also assembled a model showing the complexity of the onslaught. Many of the pillbox machine-gun posts are gone but enough remains, including a Dragon's Teeth anti-tank trap, cleared of vegetation by National Trust Warden Geoff Hann to show the obstacles that the invading soldiers had to overcome. He also has his hidden cache of wartime ordnance awaiting the next visit of the Royal Engineers' Bomb Disposal unit from Bulford Camp. 'Unexploded shells still turn up,' he told me.

Overlooking it all, now that post-war sycamores have been cleared from the edge of Redend Point, is Fort Henry, lying seawards of the lawns and paddocks of the Manor House Hotel (SZ 038 828). The largest Observation Post in Britain, with a yard of solid concrete in front, behind, above and below, it stretches 30 yards with protected compartments for batches of officers to watch and learn from the progress of this and other exercises. An eye-level

recessed slit had outer stepped protection to ricochet any stray cannon fire. The structure is just about indestructible. Concrete buildings in Hiroshima, far less solid than this, survived the atom bomb, an officer told me. Behind it is an earlier 4-inch gun battery, dated 1940 in wet cement, which was redundant by the time of the King's visit. Active aerial defence on Tuesday 18 April 1944 was provided in the manor grounds by an American battalion of mobile heavy Anti-Aircraft Artillery. They also had a watching brief for German E-boats – high speed motor-torpedo gunboats – though Exercise Smash came before the chastening debacle in Lyme Bay when hundreds were killed during the enemy interception of landing-craft heading for Slapton Sands.

Among the most amazing armoured fighting vehicles put through their paces on Studland's beach and dunes were DD – duplex-drive – Valentine light tanks which swam ashore in canvas screens. At least four failed to float in choppy conditions and sank to the seabed in Studland Bay. In theory, looking like small boats, they were inconspicuous among a mass of much larger assault landing vessels and would not therefore be targeted by enemy defenders. Crewmen, however, remained unconvinced. 'We regarded them as courting disaster,' Ron West told me. 'One shot through the canvas skirt and they would sink like a stone.'

Despite the reservations of their drivers and gunners, hundreds of Valentine and Sherman tanks were converted into DD versions and played an important part in the D-Day landings in an infantry-support role. A propeller at the rear was powered by the tank's bevel drive. The screen was raised by compressed air. On reaching land it was collapsed and the tank could then drive into action.

Studland was also chosen to test Hobart's Funnies, as the creations of Major-General Sir Percy Cleghorn Stanley Hobart (1885–1957) were known.

He raised the specialised 79th Armoured Division. One of its most effective adaptations was a Churchill tank which had its gun turret removed and replaced with an immense roll of modified canvas interwoven with chestnut fencing. This was lowered ahead of it to form a strip of carpet across the dunes. The instant road was then used by normal tanks which would otherwise have ground to a halt in the soft sand.

Offshore, in Studland Bay, one of the experimental 'Scam Projects' was put through its trials but soon abandoned due to the inherent unpredictability of wind and waves. *Lily* was the code-name for a floating airfield that was a raft just large enough for a single torpedo-carrying Swordfish biplane to be deployed in a rocket-assisted take-off.

The past lived again on 18 April 2002 when the National Trust declared Fort Henry open. Trust Dorset Area Manager David Jenkins was properly dressed as successor in title to Ralph Bankes, the last private landowner, as Vice-Admiral of Purbeck. I wore the uniform of Colonel W.H. Blagden of the Royal Engineers in tribute to the builders – though the actual construction of Fort Henry was by Canadian Engineers in 1943, and they named it for their base in Ontario. 'Prime Minister, may I ask you to declare Fort Henry officially re-opened,' I said, as the familiar figure of wartime premier Winston Churchill stepped forward with splendid trademark Cuban cigar donated by Andrew Purkis. I am told Mr Churchill can also do a passable impersonation of Weston-super-Mare actor Graham Gadd.

All three of us, and General Dwight D. Eisenhower, the Supreme Commander, Allied Expeditionary Force (courtesy the United States 1st Infantry Division Living History Company), were upstaged by an authentic local hero. Bill Chutter was born in 1914, at the start of the First World War, and was of just the right age to go through the entire repeat performance. Private Chutter went with the 1st Battalion, the Dorsetshire Regiment, to India in 1936. They then defended Malta, from 1939 to 1943, when General Montgomery welcomed them to the 8th Army and turned them into his best assault troops.

Theirs was the task of taking the beachheads in Sicily and Italy, followed by the first home leave in seven years, interrupted by Montgomery's return to Britain. As overall land-force commander for the invasion of Europe, he wanted them again on Gold Beach, on D-Day. Ironically, Bill Chutter had lost his old home, Lutton Farm between Steeple and Tyneham, which was taken over by the Army six days before Christmas in 1943, for a massive expansion of the Lulworth tank gunnery ranges.

So it was that Bill Chutter came ashore at dawn on Studland beach in Exercise Smash under the eyes of his King and General Montgomery. Churchill and Eisenhower also watched the series of assaults. Other users of binoculars in Fort Henry included Field-Marshal Sir Alan Brooke (Chief of the Imperial General Staff) and Acting Admiral Louis Mountbatten (Commander, Combined Operations).

A headquarters signalman, Bill Chutter proudly wore his campaign medals for the return to Fort Henry. He also reminded us of the reality of front-line warfare:

*There was a silent period before you pitched down and as soon as the ramp came down you had to be out very quickly. They always aimed straight at the ramp. Normandy was far worse than Italy or Sicily. I have been back to Normandy many times and wonder how we ever got through because of the number of gun positions. One hundred and four of our men were killed or wounded on the first day.*

For the American 1st Infantry Division, leaving Weymouth, Portland and Poole for Omaha Beach, the situation was far worse, with 2,000 being killed before the beachhead was secure. On the sunny day when Fort Henry made its cultural transition from unwanted eyesore to protected heritage, Bill Chutter

*Wartime Poole flying-boat* Southern Cross *returned to Studland from New Zealand in 1976 and is now an exhibit in a Southampton museum.*

*Flying-boat* Southern Cross *nearly became a Studland Bay wreck after her starboard float filled with water in 1976.*

reminded us of an uncomfortable continuity running through world history. In 1946 he had been shipped back to another war zone and found himself policing the Palestinian town of Jenin. It was again making harrowing headlines with breaking news that very day.

Those of us who only wear uniforms for fun were given several reasons to be thankful. Bill, at the age of 87 and living in Dorchester, had his close calls in India, Malta, Sicily, Italy, Normandy, the Baltic, and then pre-partition Palestine. He keeps in his wallet a folded note from Corfe Castle doctor Godfrey Dru Drury which expresses extreme concern for his childhood health. A lucky man himself, though he did not say it as such, he obviously regards us as an incredibly fortunate generation.

Of those from Studland who gave their lives in the Second World War, Lieutenant Maxwell Chenevix-Trench RE and Lieutenant Denys Wright RN have already been mentioned. The other three were Private Albert Henry Haighton of the Royal Artillery, Lance-Corporal Albert Douglas Masters of the Dorsetshire Regiment, and Sergeant Robert Humphrey Samways of the Queen's Royal Regiment.

Memories of wartime flying boats, operating from Poole Harbour throughout the conflict, including VIP flights by the British Overseas Airways Corporation to the United States and the British Empire, were dramatically revived on 24 August 1976. A 1942-built Short Sunderland Mark-3 flying boat, used in post-war New Zealand to carry the mail under the civilian

registration *ZK-AMH*, had returned to Poole as the *Southern Cross*. Her pilot was Captain Charles Blair.

On 23 August he was told to land beside Old Harry Rocks but an adverse easterly wind caused him to follow normal practice of wartime flyers and land in much calmer conditions on Poole Harbour. This was now cluttered with leisure craft but he managed to land in the Wareham Channel, near Rockley Sands, giving the authorities a surprise. The following day, having carried out a number of nostalgic flights, he was persuaded to come down on his choppy mooring in Studland Bay.

While the crew and guests visited the Bankes Arms Hotel some nautical vandal removed the flying boat's aft bilge cap from the float on the starboard wing. This caused it to take in water and sink as the port float rose into the air. Captain Ron Gillies saved the day by skilfully bringing the crippled boat between Shell Bay and Sandbanks as he followed in the wake of Channel ferry *Cherbourg* as she entered Poole Harbour. The propellers were sending up spray and the flying boat tossed in the swell as it was brought to the safety of a buoy in the shallows behind Brownsea Island.

The veteran aircraft lived to see another day, roaring off over Old Harry after repairs, and saw out her flying life in the Virgin Islands. Her charmed existence extended to retirement, being bought by the Science Museum in 1981 and put on display in Southampton Hall of Aviation when it opened in 1984.

# Chapter 10

# VILLAGE SCENES & PEOPLE

*Donkey cart and gentleman in Edwardian boater, in a shot of Beach Road by Dorchester photographer Walter Pouncy, before the building of Longmead.*

A succession of distinguished people have made themselves at home in Studland. Population details, totalling 384 in the first census of 1803, and rising to 435 in 1841, are only part of the picture. Although there were 543 people living in its 4,882 acres in 1911 the growth was underestimated by statistics as many of its devotees, like the present 20,000 users attracted to the beach every day in high summer, lived their recorded lives elsewhere. The electoral roll for 2001 lists 398 men and women over the age of 18, with a dozen of them living on Brownsea Island.

As with Swanage having its brickworks on the south side of Godlingston Hill, that at Studland was also on the edge of the community, on the south side of the main track into Studland Heath. The remains of the kilns, apparently last used in the 1890s, can still be seen as you approach Wadmore Farm. The other village facility, its Elementary School, was built in

1845 for 94 children, with 46 being the average attendance when Miss Clara Bassum was the mistress in late-Victorian times. Mrs E.A. Eastham had succeeded her by the First World War, in the time of confectioner and baker John Walker who ran the village shop beside the crossroads at The Green, 150 yards away at the west end of School Lane.

John Summers, buried under the yew tree in 1705, has the oldest decipherable inscription in the churchyard. Inside the church Frances Meaux, the daughter of Sir William Meaux, was buried in 1662. Another memorial is to Ann Beaumont, the widow of George Brown, who died in 1713. Francis Fane (1753–1813), who represented the boroughs of Lyme Regis and then Dorchester in the House of Commons for 30 years, died at Studland. His widow, Ann Fane, kept on their Studland home and died in 1832 at the age of 79.

Notable rectors include Revd Benjamin Culme,

## *Sylvan Setting*

Above: *The 'Fir Wood' on the western approach to Studland, at Woodhouse, in 1900.*

Below: *Crocus time at Studland, photographed by Edwin Dodshon on the first day of spring during the First World War, on 21 March 1915.*

Right: *Turnpike milestone, three miles from Swanage, where the public road system ended at Beach Road.*

*The lych-gate alone among the trees in Edwardian times.*

from 1718 to 1734, who married Judith Layphield. She gave him ten children and granddaughter Ann married James White who provided the family memorial on the nave wall in 1772. Ann White died in 1807.

Revd John Morton Colson (1762–1837) was the rector of Studland for 51 years but duplicated his incumbencies and died in another Dorset parish, at Piddlehinton, where he had been rector for 28 years.

Revd George Alston, Studland's rector from 1853 to 1878, lost his barrister son Edward Graham Alston (1831–72), the Queen's Advocate for the colony of Sierra Leone, 'from the fatal effects of the climate'. He died on 12 November 1872 after only a year in West Africa. On the other side of the continent, Charles Alan Smythies (1844–94) – who spent his boyhood in Studland – was the Bishop of Zanzibar from 1883. He died aboard the steamship *Peiho* and was buried at sea in the Indian Ocean on 7 May 1894.

Studland Manor represented the usually absentee landowning family, the Bankes Estate of Corfe Castle and Kingston Lacy, though their presence proliferated after its major rebuilding in 1848 by George Bankes MP (died 1856). His brother William John Bankes (1786–1855), in exile in Venice since 1841 as a result of a homosexual scandal, is said to have surreptitiously slipped ashore at Studland while delivering consignments of classical art for embellishing Kingston Lacy House. George Bankes' sons also enjoyed the family's marine villa. William Bankes, who won a posthumous VC in the Lucknow Siege, recalled sailing adventures from Studland in his dying words.

The revamped Studland Manor, despite the 1848 rebuilding, incorporates ancient walls and is an extrovert and extravagant piece of architectural fun.

Two round towers on the north-west side look as if they were inspired by those at Godlingston Manor, in the family's lands on the other side of the Purbeck Hills. On the other hand there are flourishes that may well preserve the memory of Studland Castle and mimmic other shapes and forms around Old Harry Rocks. It all makes for a chaotic roof line of dormers, turrets and appendages. Inside, the building has reused fittings, such as a Gothic landing, a fine eighteenth-century carved fireplace, and a door surround featuring Orpheus in the forest with wild animals. When rebuilding the roadside wall in 2000, National Trust property manager Julian Homer had the brilliant idea of inserting portholes to give glimpses eastwards across the grounds to Studland Bay beyond.

The foremost homes, scenically, were cliff-side residences such as Harry Warren House and Studland Bay House – previously known as Kya-Lami – where *Titanic* survivor Jacob Gibbons was head gardener. To here the Honourable Sir Eustace Fiennes (1864–1943) made his escapes from Parliament and 86 Eaton Terrace, London SW1. The MP for Banbury, knighted in 1916, he had served as a Major in the Oxfordshire Imperial Yeomanry in a succession of campaigns from Cairo to Cape Town. These included the Riel Rebellion of 1885, two campaigns in Egypt, the pioneer expedition to Mashonaland, and the Boer War to round off the century.

He went back to war in 1914 and was a general staff officer with the Royal Naval Division to the Dardanelles in the Gallipoli landings of 1915. His post-war career was as Governor of the Seychelle Islands from 1918 and Governor and Commander-in-Chief of the Leeward Islands from 1921 to retirement in 1929.

*Street scene from The Green in 1935.*

## Studland Manor

Above: *Studland Manor, the Bankes family's coastal villa, in its earliest mid-Victorian photograph.*

Below: *The chaotic roof line of Studland Manor Hotel, as rebuilt in 1848, showing its frontage from the south-west.*

## *Studland Manor*

*Towers and turrets, mimicking aspects of old Purbeck from elsewhere on the Bankes Estate, photographed from the north-west by Rodney Legg in 2002.*

Right: *Porthole view, giving an eastwards glimpse of Studland Bay, being the brilliant concept of Julian Homer for the National Trust when the roadside wall was rebuilt in 2000.*

Left: *Back view of Studland Manor Hotel, showing the south side from the grounds, in 1983.*

# Hill Close

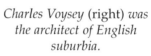

Charles Voysey (right) was the architect of English suburbia.

Hill Close, built by Arts and Crafts architect Charles Voysey for playwright Alfred Sutro, photographed by Rodney Legg in 2002.

Kenneth Anderson of Harry Warren House rented Dean Hill from landowner Walter Bankes (1853–1904) in 1892 and established the 9-hole Isle of Purbeck Golf Club which opened for play in 1893. Like all golf courses at that time it was known as 'the links'. Anderson's son was the first to win the Bankes Gold Medal in 1895.

Brigadier-General Stuart Milligan Anderson (1879–1954) of the Royal Artillery served in the Boer War and became a director of the Extel newsagency – Exchange Telegraph Company Limited – which monitored world stock markets. He married Alexandra Helen Ganesco from Bucharest in 1914. By the end of the First World War he had won both the Distinguished Service Order and its American equivalent, the Legion of Honor.

The thatched Dean Cottage was the home of Mary Ann Howe and husband Thomas Howe until their deaths in 1907 and 1909. Their son, Joseph Howe (1865–1929), was the first golf professional on the course, and his home doubled as the original clubhouse. After the death of Walter Bankes, with his son Henry John Ralph Bankes (1901–81) being too young to run the estate for a couple of decades, Major Alfred Thomas Lodder acted as clerk and agent. He was pressed to release more land to the club by Captain Metcalfe-Smith, which was agreed from Michaelmas in 1908, with the southern side of Godlingston Heath being released for an additional course on the other side of the main road. It had to be fenced to prevent Ernest Homer's cattle from straying across the new greens and his successor, Mr Drew, kept up the pressure on the club.

Initially, there were nine holes but the club soon asked for a further nine holes, and permission to build a clubhouse, 'in the event of our getting 18 holes on the heath.' The new course was laid out by H.L. Curtis from Bournemouth, across 59 acres, 2 roods, 1 perch of ground known as Broadspan. Ernest Battrick, Joseph Howe's nephew from Rempstone, was the first groundsman.

Sir Eyre Crowe (1864–1925) spent his holidays in Studland with his wife Clema von Bonin (1869–1953), the eldest daughter of Professor Gerhardt. Sir Eyre rose through the ranks at the Foreign Office from clerk in 1885 to permanent under-secretary of state for foreign affairs in 1920. Their son Eric Eyre Crowe (1905–52) entered the diplomatic service and was political secretary to the high commissioner in South Africa at the end of the Second World War. The other Crowe children were Asta (1903–53), Una (1906–26) and Sibyl (1908–93).

The playwright Alfred Sutro

*Art expert Sir Herbert Cook of Hill Close at Studland.*

(1863–1933) adopted Studland early in his career and had Hill Close built at Woodhouse Hill as his studio-style holiday home in 1896. He was then working with Arthur Bourchier on a joint adaptation of the *Chilli Widow*. Sutro went on to have highly successful plays running in the West End for the next three decades. He saw one or two new productions on to the stage every year. Some endured and in popularity he was second only to Sir Arthur Pinero though his fame would die with him. Few now can recall his works. They included *The Cave of Illusion* (1900), *Arethusa* (1903), *A Marriage has been Arranged* and *The Walls of Jerico* (1904), *The Perfect Lover* (1905), *The Fascinating Mr Vanderveldt* (1906), *John Glaydes's Honour* and *The Barrier* (1907), *The Builder of Bridges* (1908), *Making a Gentleman* (1909), *The Perplexed Husband* (1911), *The Fire-Screen* (1912), *The Two Virtues* and *The Clever Ones* (1914), *Uncle Anyhow* (1918), *The Choice* (1919), *The Laughing Lady* and *The Great Well* (1922), *The Desperate Lovers* (1927), and *Living Together* (1929). He also translated Maeterlinck's *Wisdom and Destiny* and *Life of the Bee*.

Arts and Crafts architect Charles Francis Annesley Voysey (1857–1941) created one of his acclaimed houses for Alfred Sutro at Hill Close. It is a six-bedroom listed building, noted for its architectural interest, with a matching garden of stone walls, contoured mounds and seaside views that shows the influence of Gertrude Jekyll and Thomas Mawson. Interior features, at different levels, include plaster friezes and wooden balconies, beneath deep roofs and rough-cast walls with asymmetrical placing of windows and chimneys. Repose, harmony, cheerfulness, comfort, warmth, quietness and ease of upkeep were among the watch-words in a design that exuded confidence by providing 'a frame to its inmates' in a setting that demanded attention, 'so rich and poor alike will appreciate its qualities.'

Art connoisseur and writer Sir Herbert Cook (1868–1939), the second baronet, was the son of Sir Frederick Cook. He married the Honourable Mary Hood, the eldest daughter of the 2nd Viscount Bridport, and bought Hill Close at Studland. Vera Cook, their daughter, married Major Dudley Ryder, the head of the Ryder family at Rempstone Hall. She recalled that her father discovered the delights of Studland in the summer of 1908 and returned for 'every ensuing holiday'. Sir Herbert was the chairman of Cook, Son and Company of St Paul's and a trustee of several cultural institutions, including the National Portrait Gallery and the National Gallery, as well as being a founder of the National Art Collections Fund.

## Bloomsbury Group

*Virginia Woolf, introduced to Studland by George Bernard Shaw, brought her friends and scandalised the village. She is pictured (above) in Studland in 1910.*

*Cliff End, the Edwardian villa remembered for Studland's visitors from Bloomsbury, photographed by Colin Graham in 1984.*

While checking his details I spotted a reference to Scottish artist Edwin Alexander (1870–1926) having painted in Studland. I then recalled writing about his painting Mrs Alexander and young May Worley Morton beside Nos 2 and 3 Watery Lane. She told me that the Alexanders had a black servant and that Antarctic explorer Captain Robert Falcon Scott (1868–1912) stayed with them at Studland before departing on his last great adventure in the Terra Nova. The other coincidence that day was that I came across a report that a Captian Scott from Studland was convicted of driving a motor car at 'excessive speed' at Swanage in 1909. This was 'more that 19 miles an hour' and he failed to produce his licence. Captain Scott was fined £2 with 19s. costs.

Studland's Victorian ladies were scandalised after the turn of the century as the village achieved the status of Bloomsbury-by-Sea. London's intellectual free spirits became conspicuous after the arrival of sisters Vanessa and Virginia Stephen. Their respective married partners were the art critic Clive Bell and Fabian historian Leonard Woolf. Vanessa and Virginia were recommended to visit Studland by friend and playwright George Bernard Shaw who had discovered Shell Bay in 1901 when he was staying in the Chine Hotel, Bournemouth.

The Bloomsbury set included novelist E.M. Forster, essayist Lytton Strachey, painter Roger Fry, and artist Duncan Grant. They were said to 'live in squares and love in triangles'. One of the triangular relationships that came about at Studland was a room for Roger Fry courtesy Clive and Vanessa Bell. Roger and Vanessa soon became lovers.

Virginia Woolf rented a succession of Studland houses from 1909 to 1913 including The Cottage, 2 Harmony Cottages and Harbour View. 'Julian rushes straight into the sea,' she wrote, going on to say:

*Nessa tacks her skirt up. Clive dives from a boat in a tight black suit. Yesterday I hired a gentleman's bi-sexual bathing dress, and swam far out, until the seagulls played over my head.*

Another triangular relationship centred on Cliff End, an Edwardian villa in the trees between the Bankes Arms and South Beach, which was rented by Philip Morrell (1870–1943), the Liberal MP for Burnley. During the Easter holiday of 1911, Cliff End was the setting for the seduction of Morrell's

*Ben Pond rowing his boat,* Tam, *in the 1920s.*

wife, Lady Ottoline Morrell, by mathematician and philosopher the Honourable Bertrand Russell (1872–1970). The former Lady Ottoline Cavendish-Bentinck, half-sister of the 6th Duke of Portland, remained Russell's mistress for several years, in an affair that simmered until 1916 when Russell was dismissed from his post at Trinity College, Cambridge, for pacifist opposition to the First World War. Bertrand became the 3rd Earl Russell on the death of his elder brother in 1931.

'She gave me less and less,' Russell complained about Ottoline, 'while at the same time she gave more and more to others.' He was particularly miffed that though he was no longer allowed to enter her bedroom 'Aldous Huxley was habitually present while she undressed.' With hair 'like that of marmalade, though rather darker', the tall, svelte form of Ottoline Morrell was immortalised as Hermione Roddice in D.H. Lawrence's *Women in Love* (1920). She then starred in Huxley's *Crome Yellow* (1921).

A longer-term Studland arrival was the artist and globe-trotter Alexander Berens who bought a cottage between Beach Road and Ferry Road in 1902. He called it Full Stop and began a gentrification that turned his home into a mansion now known as Sandyholme. Berens admired the pioneering Scout camp held by Robert Baden-Powell on Brownsea Island and inaugurated his own Studland troop. He claimed to have marshalled his own 'Army' of 200 boys and took them into the heath on 'camp-craft expeditions'. Sandyholme began to look increasingly Morrocan, with doorways shaped as Moorish keyholes and hung with embroidery and tooled leather. He created an enterprise called Studland Art Industries which attracted a succession of 'peculiar people' to the village.

Wild Man No. 1, a tramp, lived in derelict Curlew Cottages, in a clump of scrub midway along the South Haven peninsula about a mile south-west of Shell Bay. He slept on a bed of heather. Having lived among the Crees, in Canada, he described vivid memories of those times and brought them to life with representations of Red Indians in chalk crayon around the cottage walls. The figures were life size. Their fires and wigwams were depicted to a background of snowy mountains.

Wild Man No. 2 was itinerant boatman and beachcomber Benjamin Pond who ran errands around Poole Harbour and lived in an old clay-worker's hut on Newton Heath. The two would tell stories of each other and once spent a frightening night together in Curlew Cottages without realising the other was there. Ben Pond had gone by train from Poole to Blandford to visit a cousin. He returned from across Poole Harbour with a bulging bag of books and produce and moored his boat at South Haven:

*Dark clouds overspread the Purbeck sky and darker still was the track through the tall heather. Had gone about a mile when a few drops of rain began to fall; a thunderstorm was not faraway. Yes, Curlew Cottages. I could seek shelter there. I did not wish my books and eatables to get wet.*

Wild Man No. 1 had been gone for years and Pond expected to be alone. He was only mildly disturbed as piercing Red Indian eyes, illuminated by each lightning flash, followed him around the room. Boughs of trees rubbed Brontë-style against the windows:

*I had entered the room without a qualm of fear, but now I was shivering like a jelly. Somewhere in the room above there came a heavy thud, causing me to break into a sweat, and a minute or so later there came a second thud. I could stand no more and out into the fury of the storm I dashed. My clothes got torn by brambles, my books and shopping I left where they fell, and never was I so glad to reach my little shack as I was that awful night.*

Next morning he realised the human dimension to his ghost of Curlew Cottage when Scott, the ferryman at South Haven, told him: 'Tramp bloke is back. Bin away over seven years and now bin back up Curlew a week. Already owes me for two crossings.'

Wild Man No. 1 confirmed the story, telling how as he went to bed someone swept out of the house into the storm, and left him too scared to move till daybreak. When he eventually ventured out he had his reward: 'I found books an' bags of grub in the bushes, beachcombing on me doorstep, as you might say.'

After the First World War, when Knoll House was rented by the economist Maynard Keynes, Leonard and Virginia Woolf returned to Studland. Robert Graves followed. The older buildings on Knowl Hill, now Knoll House Hotel, were built by Walter Bankes in 1905 as a summer-house for Alfred Douglas Douglas-Hamilton, 13th Duke of Hamilton (1862–1940) of Ferne House, Shaftesbury. His son and heir Douglas Douglas-Hamilton, 14th Duke of Hamilton (1903–1973), a pilot in the Royal Air Force, headed the Everest Flight Expedition in 1933. Early in the Second World War he had his name borrowed by MI6 for a lengthy correspondence with Hitler's deputy, Rudolf Hess, leading to his defection to the Duke's Scottish estate in Lanarkshire on 11 May 1941. The German leader had been duped into believing he could make peace with an anti-Churchill faction.

*Knoll House Hotel, seen from the east in 2000, was the holiday home of the Duke of Hamilton.*

# Village People

*Young Edwardian recruits forming a 'Band of Hope' for the Studland branch of the Church of England Temperance Society.*

Above: *Victorian studio portrait, from London's Edgware Road, of Studland villagers Gus and Mabel Payne.*

Above: *Charles and Mary Ann Payne at Watery Lane Cottages.*

Right: *Revd Frederick Swift Algeo, the rector from 1892 to 1923* (seated, centre), *with his Village Hall Committee.*

## Village Views

Left: *Beach Road and Longmead (centre) in 1959.*

Below, inset: *Studland Post Office was in a new Victorian villa in Swanage Road (right).*

Above: *Steppes Pond and Beach Road forming a green approach to Middle Beach in 1905.*

Right: *The Victorian section of the churchyard.*

## Village Views

By 1908 the humble home on Dean Hill had become Golf Cottage.

The cottage between the Bankes Arms and Manor House to which
Waterloo veteran Sergeant William Lawrence retired.

Inset: Wadmore Farm, beyond the Victorian brick works on the edge of Studland Heath,
photographed by Rodney Legg in 2000.

## Village Views

Colonel Hynes's house
in the 1920s.

Right: *The Swanage Road entrance to Studland village, from the south-west, sketched by F. Hibbert in 1919.*

STUDLAND VILLAGE
JUNE 1919

Left: *Rare postcard view of what was modern Studland in 1930.*

*A motor car parked in Swanage Road in the 1930s.*

## Village Views

Right: *Ballard Down as the backdrop to Manor Farm, southwards from the Church Road junction in 1983.*

Left and below: *Church Cottage, looking westwards from the cliff-top pastures between Manor Road and South Beach.*

*Holme-Dene, Manor Road, is the home of Mrs Doreen White, licensee of the Fox Inn at Corfe Castle.*

*Beach Road and Beach Cottage, from the south-east, photographed by Colin Graham in 1983.*

*Left: Beach Cottage, with butterfly-friendly flora, photographed from the east by Rodney Legg in 2000.*

The Douglas-Hamiltons deserted Studland in 1924 when it became clear that an influx of cars and charabancs were inevitable once the Ferry Company started operations in 1926.

Knoll House Hotel was created in 1930 when the buildings were revamped by Dorchester hoteliers Christopher and Poppy Smith. They paid the Bankes Estate £225 per annum rent and then bought the free-hold for £7,000. It opened for business, at £6.6s.0d. a week, on 31 March 1931. There were initially only a few bedrooms.

Cliff End went from Bloomsbury notoriety to military respectability, as the home of an eighth baronet, Colonel Sir Harry Llewellyn Mackworth (1878–1952) who was awarded the Distinguished Service Order in the Boer War. Serving with the Royal Corps of Signals and later attached to the Royal Engineers, he took part in the Gallipoli landings in the Dardanelles in 1915 and retired to Cliff End in 1927.

In 1939, George Mervyn Anstey Hamilton-Fletcher was living at the Manor House, before it became an hotel. Lieutenant-Colonel Neville Gardner ran Knoll Riding School. Brigadier-General S.M. Anderson was living in Harry Warren House. Cyril Conners was at High Hedges. James Fluker was at Kinross. Augustus Granville-White lived at Woodend. J.H. MacMillan was in Studland Bay House. Ernest George Woodward was in Woodgate Lodge.

Leading ladies in the community were Miss Allen at Sweet Briar; the Honourable Lady Cook in Hill Close; Mrs Norman Cowie at Varhn; Mrs Guppy in Greengates; Mrs Ernest Leathers in Wyards; Miss Mayo at Swallow Cliffe; Mrs Murray-Tosh in Corner Cottage; Mrs Stobart-Greenhalgh in

Knapwynd; Lady Thomson in Studholm; and Mrs Elsa Winzia in Homeland.

After the Second World War the ashes of novelist and futurist Herbert George Wells (1866–1946), who is best remembered for *The War of the Worlds* in which Martian spacecraft land on common land near Woking, were cast into the sea off Old Harry Rocks. He produced science fiction for half a century, from *The Time Machine* (1895) to *The Shape of Things to Come* (1933), *The New World Order* (1940) and *The Phoenix* (1942). Radical works included *Ann Veronica* (1909) which promoted feminism. Pot-boilers were issued under the pseudonym Reginald Bliss.

At his memorial service, a passage was read from his work which concluded: 'We are all things that make and pass, striving upon a hidden mission, out to the open sea.'

This persuaded his family to have his ashes scattered at sea. Son Anthony and half-brother Gip chartered the *Deidre* from Poole Quay. They found themselves 'pitching badly' off the Bar, beyond the harbour entrance. Anthony recalled the moment for his father's biographer, Anthony West:

*The wind took them off as a long veil that struck the pale green waves with a hiss. The* Deidre *wallowed as Captain Miller put her about and I had a moment of agony. He was really gone now.*

Sir Newman Flower (1879–1964), rooted in Dorset at Fontmell Magna and Tarrant Keynston, had been Wells' publisher at Cassells. He remembered him as a 'most untidy writer' who filled the margins of his manuscripts with afterthoughts that would collide. Each was in a 'balloon' and lines trailed across the

# Cross Tree

Above: *Brilliantly clear Victorian photograph of the Cross Tree in 1895 enabling its public notice to be read:*
*'Any persons stealing ferns, sand, earth or peat, will be prosecuted without further notice.'*

Below: *Working horses beside the Cross Tree in a view south-eastwards to the dairy at*
*Manor Farm in 1902.*

# Cross Tree

*Edwardian watercolour showing the Cross Tree beside the rustic cart shed.*

# Cross Tree

Right: *Pre-1908 photograph of Studland's most picturesque corner, showing Studland Dairy behind the Cross Tree.*

Below: *Bystanders at the Cross Tree as fire devastates the dairy at Manor Farm on 8 August 1908.*

*Fordson tractor in the cart shed, in 2002, with the tree gone and the cross restored.*

## *The Green*

Above: *Carts on The Green in about 1900.*

Right: *The Cottage on The Green in 1906.*

*John Walker's shop, beside the crossroads at The Green, seen in a view eastwards into School Lane in 1912.*

# The Green

Above: *The rural idyll in Heath Green Lane in 1913.*

Left: *New houses on The Green, designed by Alexander Hamilton-Fletcher, with the 1993-dated stone by the tree being for Studland's 'Best Kept Village' award.*

Right: *Studland Stores in a view from across the road, in 1995.*

## Studland Cottages

Above: *Victorian watercolour of cottages in Watery Lane.*

Below: *Vine Cottage with its extension* (right) *trading as 'Ye Olde Shoppe'.*

# Vine Cottage

Above: *Vine Cottage was the home of the Payne family of Studland boatmen.*

*Lizzie Payne* (left) *and Mary Ann Payne at Vine Cottage.*

*The shop beside Vine Cottage.*

# Watery Lane

*Watery Lane at its most rustic, in 1890, became the most photographed corner of the village.*

# Watery Lane

Top photograph:
*Old oaks, living and felled,
in Watery Lane in the 1890s.*

Left: *Cottages in
Watery Lane in 1890.*

# Watery Lane

Above: *Victorian photograph taken in 1895 of the picturesque corner in Watery Lane.*

Above: *Watery Lane cottages in 1904.*

Left: *Cottage in Watery Lane in 1902.*

page to show where they were to be inserted. Wells, however, was more than a match for Flower's strictures:

*I sell my books to Flower,*
*I give my books to Flower,*
*He kicks and beats me, drives me, starves me;*
*He has me in his power.*

*Christian, dost thou hear him?*
*He prowls, and prowls, and prowls!*
*Still, I give my books to Flower.*

Management of the golf links, which had changed its name from Isle of Purbeck Golf Club to Swanage and Studland Golf Club, was assigned by Brigadier-General Anderson in 1946 to businessman Harry Palmer of Chalfont Park, Buckinghamshire. He had a seaside flat looking across to the Purbeck Hills from Bath Hill Court, Bournemouth. Having obtained permission from the Bankes Estate to move the clubhouse to the north side of the Corfe–Studland road, as had been mooted a couple of decades before, he changed the name to Studland Bay Golf. Ralph Bankes approved the building of the new clubhouse but refused to relinquish or restrict his shooting rights, and vetoed a request for tennis courts and a bowling green.

The postwar bulge in the birth rate came too late to save the village school. Parents preferred to send their children across the hill to Mount Scar in Swanage with the exception of Mrs Edith Summers who argued that younger children should stay in the village. Elizabeth Summers, her youngest daughter, was the one and only pupil remaining in Studland School when it closed in 1947. She then attended St Mark's Church of England School in Herston. The wisdom of closing village schools was questioned again in the 1970s after a young girl was killed by a car in Swanage Road at Studland on arriving home in the school bus.

Of all the literati who passed through Studland, it is no longer any contest to name the two who are best known to adults and children of all ages. Enid Blyton, the best-selling English author of the twentieth century, produced more than 700 books. All are full of exclamation marks and most are said to have a Purbeck-related line to the effect that 'there is a light out at sea'. While staying at the Hotel Grosvenor in Swanage she became sponsor of the town's Regatta and Carnival and told of her connections with the town:

*My daughters and I always spend our holidays in Swanage. I also write here while my husband plays golf. I think straight on to my typewriter. It's the best way of writing vividly* [exclamation mark deleted].

She watched the shipping from the Isle of Purbeck Golf Course and discovered Studland policeman Christopher Rone (1915–90). Coming over the hill on his bicycle was the archetypal village Bobby, as constables had been known since their institution by Sir Robert Peel, and this one was about to give his colleagues a new generic name. A podgy ex-Guardsman, Christopher Rone became Enid Blyton's model for PC Plod in the Noddy stories from Toytown. Years later, on hearing of his claim to fame from Swanage reporter George Willey, he proceeded to dine out on it with pride.

*The Bankes Arms in 1930.*

By then in retirement, at Carey Close in Wareham, he enjoyed the attribution for the rest of his life and received an obituary in more than one national newspaper.

Enid Blyton and her husband, Harley Street surgeon Kenneth Darrell-Waters, bought the Isle of Purbeck Golf Club in 1951 – for a token £1 note as it languished in the doldrums of austerity – and remained in charge until 1965. Miss Blyton occasionally worked on her books on a table outside the clubhouse, then affectionately known as the 'little tin hut', as K. Merle Chacksfield records in the club's centenary publication *100 Years of Golf on the Isle of Purbeck* (1992). This clubhouse stood on the west side of the Studland to Swanage road at Dean Hill, a short distance past the fork leading uphill towards Corfe Castle, on Bankes Estate land that in the opening years of the twenty-first century is owned by the National Trust.

Colonel Kenneth Ferguson bought Knoll House Hotel in the hot summer of 1959 and groomed his sons Michael and Christopher to succeed him. Post-war austerity was at last receding into memory as Studland beach enjoyed its busiest year of the new Elizabethan age. A long-remembered highlight was its adoption by Swanage Swimming Club for their polo playing. Purbeck's top team comprised Phil Bird, Mike Bond, Richard Caldwell, George Crane, Gilles Remy, 'Sully' Sullivan, Alan Vince and George Willey.

The golf course was acquired by Harry Beckham Randolph, head of blade-making family firm Wilkinson Sword Limited, in 1965. He delegated its management to his aide Bertram Aber, set about mending personal relationships with landowner Ralph Bankes, and restored its name to the Isle of Purbeck Golf Club. The hopes of half a century earlier came into effect on the ground, with a total of 27 holes. The Purbeck Course of 18 holes is north of the Corfe-Studland road and the original 9 holes on Dean Hill are known as the Dene Course.

A modern clubhouse was provided at last. Designed by John Burgess Associates and built by Albert Marsh, both from Wareham, it opened at Christmas 1966 with a copper roof on top and Purbeck stone fossils inside. Swords appeared, everywhere, adorning the walls both as decoration and trophies for tournaments. They included a replica Stalingrad Sword, commemorating the wartime resistance of the Russian people, and a copy of Emperor Haile Selassie of Ethiopia's Gold Flaming Sword. Wilkinson Sword's two-millionth bayonet was also presented to the club. Soon there was a Randolph Sword, Purbeck Sword and Anchor Sword to play for, with the latter being given to customers at the Anchor Inn in the High Street at Swanage. The 'Sword Bar' and restaurant were added in 1974.

Studland fisherman David Sales, the skipper of Purbeck Isle, came home with an archetypal fisherman's tale on 18 June 1975 after venturing into the Royal Navy's gunnery range in the English Channel, thinking it was safe to do so:

*A shell landed 75 yards behind the boat. Then another shell landed less than 50 yards away. I was really concerned then – I thought the next shell might hit me amidships. I got straight on to the radio and put an emergency call through to Niton – Coastguard area headquarters – and told them I was under gunfire. They put out an alarm and the Coastguard at Wyke Regis said he would handle the situation. He must have moved pretty quickly because he got on to the Navy and five minutes later was able to tell me it was a NATO exercise involving gunnery practice. The ship that fired near my position was, in fact, a German vessel.*

It was during the Ford-Brezhnev stage of the Cold War and the Allied Commander-in-Chief Channel was Admiral Sir Henry Leach. David Sales was infuriated to hear that the Navy regarded it as 'a fishy story' and counter-attacked by saying they had been known to land shells in Chapman's Pool, Worth Matravers and Langton Matravers. A retired old salt reminded him that it was not unknown for innocent fishermen to be killed in peacetime. He instanced the Russian interception of Hull's fishing fleet, in the North Sea on 22 October 1906, thinking they were Japanese warships that had sailed around the globe for a sneak attack.

Up at the golf club, secretary Harry Sales handed over to Colonel Sandy Wilson in 1976. The Ladies' Dorset Sword was presented by Peggy Randolph in 1979. Denys and Roy Randolph, sons of H.B. Randolph and his first wife Margaret, sold the enterprise to Midlands businessman J. Leonard Robinson in 1984. Swanage historian Merle Chacksfield has captured the moment, which typifies the 'boy-toy' nature of golf course ownership, as told by Mrs Joan Robinson: 'He was like a boy being offered a sweet shop.'

They had headed south immediately, arrived at Studland in the evening, and were 'bowled over' to see the beauty of the landscape in the evening. He refurbished the bars in 1989 and handed over the hands-on running of the golf course to sons Duncan and Keith. Howard Singleton, the oldest member of the club, celebrated his ninetieth birthday in the centenary year of 1992. Having been captain of the Society of Dorset Captains, and captain and president of the Isle of Purbeck Golf Club since 1971, he never underestimated the home challenge. 'It's a remarkably fine course,' he told Merle Chacksfield, 'and a difficult one. Every hole is a potential disaster!'

The names of the holes on the main course sum up the scenery and topography:

# The Bankes Arms

Above: *Creeper-clad view of the Bankes Arms, from the north-west in 2002.*

Right: *The feudal past hangs from a sign.*

*Street view from the south-east.*

# The Bankes Arms

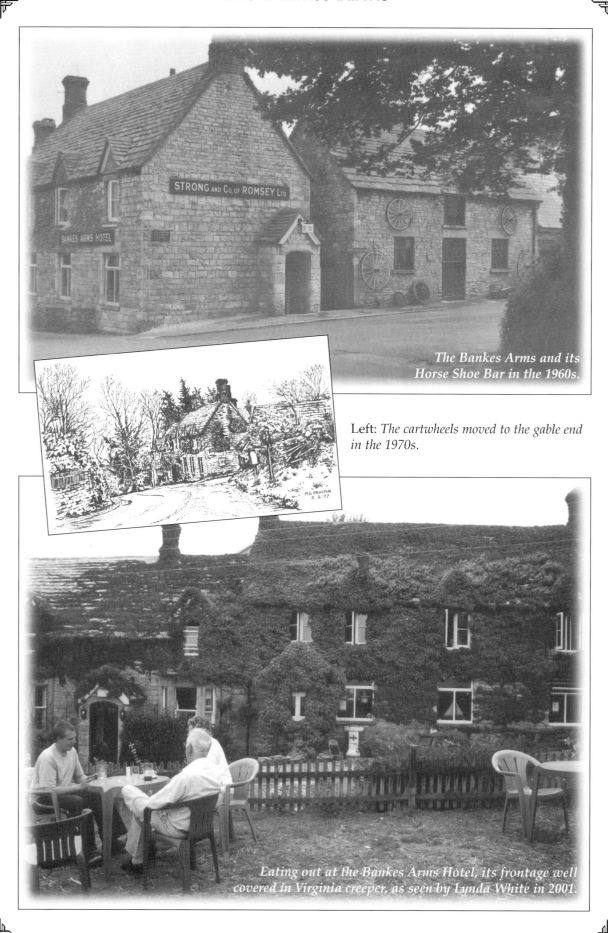

*The Bankes Arms and its
Horse Shoe Bar in the 1960s.*

Left: *The cartwheels moved to the gable end
in the 1970s.*

*Eating out at the Bankes Arms Hotel, its frontage well
covered in Virginia creeper, as seen by Lynda White in 2001.*

1st, The Dell, 371 yards.
2nd, Bankes, 417 yards.
3rd, Quarry, 302 yards.
4th, Tubbs, 195 yards.
5th, Agglestone, 404 yards.
6th, Old Harry, 492 yards.
7th, Fishing Barrow, 355 yards.
8th, Thorny Barrow, 594 yards.
9th, Punch Bowl, 147 yards.
10th, The Narrows, 414 yards.
11th, The Island, 194 yards.
12th, Tumuli, 424 yards.
13th, The Dyke, 388 yards.
14th, Rowbarrow, 389 yards.
15th, Crater, 187 yards.
16th, Cresta, 382 yards.
17th, Himalayas, 334 yards.
18th, Rhodes, 306 yards.

The 'Studland bed' on display in Dorchester was donated to Dorset County Museum by Mrs G.A. Bowyer of The Cottage on The Green in 1972. She had inherited it from Mrs Emmalette Parker (1878–1970) who lived in a seventeenth-century cob and thatch cottage next door. Mrs Bowyer told me its story:

*It was said that the bed had lived there since the cottage was built. Mrs Parker's grandmother said it had always been in the house. Their memories went back to 1800. It is an oak half-tester, 6 feet long by 4*

*feet 6 inches wide, with a tall elm headboard. They say it could have had other high sides and been semi-covered with material. The springs are squares of rope. The mattress, a bit fragile now, is of thickly-plaited golden brown rushes provided by sedge-cutters on the moors. We always looked on it as living history where villagers have slept for centuries.*

A new era for the Bankes Arms Hotel began in 1984 with the arrival of Jenny and Tim Lightbown and their sons Bill, Jack and Joe. Bill Lightbown became the home-grown chef, with seafood and game being the distinctive local dishes, and his father established an annual beer festival. He has taken an increasing interest in the practicalities of self-brewing, inspired by tales of Swanage Pale Ale, which was legendary in living memory as the local pint from over the hill.

Studland's village green is a fifth of an acre of grass and specimen trees opposite the village hall at the crossroads of Heath Green Road and School Lane with the main Swanage Road. Owned by the National Trust, and legally protected as registered unit VG 37, it is overlooked by a row of modern cottages, in red brick with dormers, which won acclaim for architect Alexander Hamilton-Fletcher in 1991.

Geoffrey Farrell, of Steppes Pond Cottage in Beach Road, told me in 1992 about a recent parish meeting in which the naming (or re-naming) of Manor Road was broached. A road sign had been lost and chairman Pat Vine decided that Rectory Lane was 'apparently its

*'Studland Parsonage' as it was when George Alston became rector in 1853, in a pen and wash sketch by C.M. Colvile.*

proper title'. Somehow my writings were used to advance claims, including that of historic Steppes Lane which still gives its name to Steppes Pond Cottage but has been displaced by the prosaic but topographically understandable Beach Road. Looking at the electoral roll, it seems that Beach Road was unassailable, but Manor Road has lost ground as Ethel and Francis Glass at the Old Rectory, along with Bonita and Richard Whitham at Rectory Cottage and the residents of Stable Cottage are living in Rectory Lane. Manor Road, however, remains writ large. Its buildings are Church Cottage, Holme Dene, Bankes Arms Hotel, Woodend House, Manor House Hotel, Pippin Cottage and Manor Cottage. Both Manor Road and Rectory Lane share the postcode BH19 3AU.

The Parish Council which had its usual preoccupation with vandalised playing-field fencing – repaired once again by Sid Churchill – received a briefing from David Stacy of Purbeck District Council on the new litter laws. In the chairman's words:

*After a most interesting discourse and many questions the situation as far as Studland is concerned was made clearer. We now have a daily visit from a lady from Wareham who is responsible for keeping Studland free from litter. Any complaints or reports from anyone will be favourably received and dealt with.*

In 1995 the preoccupation was with telecommunications, resulting from a headline in *The Times* on 22 February: 'BT 'loses' Dorset village'. The story read:

*The Dorset village of Studland has ceased to exist, according to British Telecom. All 500 inhabitants with 211 residential and 39 business telephone lines have been omitted from this year's Bournemouth area telephone directory. British Telecom regretted the error but said printing a new directory was not feasible.*

The parish's first building for the third millennium was appropriately futuristic but also environmentally friendly. It is also worthy of further research, and will no doubt receive it, being the Studland Study Centre which the National Trust has provided for children and adults. Built between the dunes and sallow scrub immediately inland from Knoll Beach car park (SZ 033 836), it is raised from the ground on a timber platform. 'The idea is that it is parked on the landscape rather than being part of it,' Trust property manager Julian Homer explained:

*It could be removed and you would almost never know it had been on the site. There's no guttering so water trickles down from the eaves on to gravel, as it falls, rather than being collected into gutters and presenting a disposal problem. In design and construction it shows how a building can be sustainable with smart-glass to keep in instant warmth, a wind-turbine for electricity, solar power for back-up, and the stove giving off maximum heat from windfall wood of which we have plenty. It's a comfortable building with nutrient-recycling water and waste management to ensure it has minimal impact on the environment.*

The exhausting catalogue of subjects embraced by Studland Study Centre includes creative writing. A study in itself, it was the setting for completion of this book, as proofs spread across the floor before going to that great filing cabinet in the sky.

*Studland's Fancy Fair in December 1920 with Elsa Winzar as Father Christmas* (left).
Left to right, back row: *Lizzie Payne, Mary Ann Payne, Mabel Payne and Lucy Ryall;*
front: *Mrs E.A. Knight and Lucy Clark.*

# Studland Performers

Above: *Swanage photographer Joan Muspratt's print of Studland pirates offering a selection of 'Girls for Sale' with 'Non-Europeans Only' being the small print.*

*Elsie Frith (left) and Elsa Winzar carting off a comrade from the Women's Institute in the Studland Pageant.*

# Celebration Time

Above: *Empire Day being marked by Studland Sunday School after the First World War.*

Below: *Coronation car for George VI's celebrations in Studland,
with Elsa Winzar and Eileen Ryall, in 1937.*

# At Play

*Five-a-side winners in 1936.*

Below: *Studland Football Club with their sponsor, J.H. Macmillan* (right), *at Studland Bay House.*

# At Play

Above: *Flower show winner Michael Clarke receives the cup from Mrs Elizabeth Payne, watched by Colin Guppy and builder Eddie Loveless (right).*

Left: *Mrs Payne also presented prizes to Kathleen Brownsea and Eddie Loveless, who had been attempting to win a cup for 32 years.*

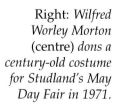

Right: *Wilfred Worley Morton (centre) dons a century-old costume for Studland's May Day Fair in 1971.*

## At Play

Above: *Bathing beauties 1970-style at Studland Regatta.*

Right: *Prize-winners Liliana Anderson* (right) *and Rosemary Payne.*

Below: *Studland's alpha male in 1973 was Stephen Rutherford* (centre) *who won the pancake race.*

# Beach Parties

Right: *Studland Pier and Redend
Point in a view from 1936 showing
that seaweed washed up on Middle
Beach is nothing new.*

**Beach and bathing huts fronting Middle
Beach in the 1920s.**

**Middle Beach Café in 1935.**

## Beach Parties

*Low water off Redend Point on a busy boating day.*

*Lady on a lilo in a peaceful scene off Middle Beach,*
*towards Studland Pier and Redend Point, in the 1930s.*

*Edwardian yachtsman, dog-walker and picnickers beside Redend Point.*

# Beach Parties

*The slippery way into Studland Bay, across kelp-covered rocks off Redend Point, now returning as history repeats itself.*

Below: *Boats and bathers on South Beach in 1956.*

## — Beach Parties —

Left: *Fully-rigged sailing boat crossing Studland Bay, seen from the Swanage side of Old Harry.*

Below: *Low-tide view of the rocks at Redend Point, southwards from Middle Beach to South Beach.*

## Beach Parties

**Front-line beach huts in the 1950s, before an advancing shoreline caused their retreat from Studland Bay.**

Below: *Bathing and boating at South Beach.*

# Fish Tales

Left: *Boats on a deserted South Beach.*

*Calm sea but hardly a prosperous voyage for the Masters and Payne family boatmen on South Beach in the 1930s.*

*Middle Beach and Studland Pier with boatmen Walter Masters (standing), Wilfred Morton and Bill Gibbons (right), in 1936.*

# Fish Tales

*Gus Payne, whose father – Charles Payne – started the family's boating business at Studland in 1885.*

Right: *Studland Bay setting as an illustration for Thomas Hardy's works: 'Well, what do you think of my poems?'*

**Boatman Albert Payne (left) with father Charles making a point on South Beach in 1932.**

# Studland Regatta

*Boatman Gus Payne with Louis Churchill and a friend at a Studland Regatta between the wars.*

*Coronation boating, celebrating the second Elizabethan age in 1953,
as the seaside returned to life following years of war and austerity.*

# Studland Regatta

*South Beach with standing room only for the Studland Regatta.*

Left: *Arrivals for the Regatta assembling below Redend Point.*

Below: *Polo players on Studland beach in the hot summer of 1959. Left to right: George Crane, Gilles Remy, Phil Bird, Mike Bond, 'Sully' Sullivan, George Willey, Richard Caldwell and Alan Vince.*

# Chapter 11

# NATURE & THE NATIONAL TRUST

*National Trust omega sign on the western approach to Studland village, on Woodhouse Hill, photographed by Rodney Legg in 1995.*

The saving of Studland for the nation came about through the overlapping enthusiasms of two central characters. Landowner Henry John Ralph Bankes (1902–81), managing his 16,000-acre estate from Kingston Lacy House in the Stour Valley between Wimborne and Badbury Rings, fortunately failed to follow his father's lead. Walter Ralph Bankes (1853–1904) died before he could help put into effect the Edwardian plan for an overhead cable-car transit system between Sandbanks and Shell Bay. Control of the estate lacked positive direction until Ralph Bankes, as the son was known, was old enough to take command. He rejected schemes for developing Shell Bay and Studland, which could so easily have turned into a second Sandbanks and Canford Cliffs, with a formidable flourish of dismissive gestures which owed a lot to the powerful influence of Captain Cyril Roper Pollock Diver (1892–1969).

After being wounded in action and sent home disabled towards the end of the First World War, Cyril Diver became an assistant clerk to the House of Commons, and finally departed from Parliament three decades later, as Clerk of Committees in 1948. Living beside Frensham Ponds in the Surrey heaths, he began assembling masses of ecological and wildlife records. Genetic and ecological researches drew him south-westwards, to Studland, where the wider habitat of coastal heathlands in a benign climate enabled him to gather records from a more productive canvas. Throughout the 1930s he visited Studland, mapping the distribution of the Dorset heath, *Erica ciliaris*, noting the evolution of dune sequences, studying banded snails, and collecting grasshoppers. He shared his knowledge of Purbeck plants with Professor Ronald D'Oyley Good (1896–1992), the head of botany at Hull University from 1928 till 1959. An old boy of Weymouth

College, who moved to Parkstone, Good also came across on the ferry, to see how many of the locations recorded by Victorian naturalist Edmund Mansel-Pleydell were still performing botanically. The heath grasshopper was identified as a separate species from specimens found 'near Swanage' in 1922 but fortunately Captain Diver's notes were much more specific and enabled John Breeds, Bunny Teagle and Rees Cox to re-find it almost immediately in the vicinity of the Observation Post, between Greenland and Little Sea, in both short and lanky heather. Rees Cox told me of their excitement:

*Once we got our eyes and ears synchronised for the stridulation we then found several other pockets of population, 20 or 30 metres apart.*

Publication in 1947 by the Ministry of Town and Country Planning of command paper 7122, on *Conservation and Nature in England and Wales*, led to wildlife protection measures being incorporated into the National Parks and Access to the Countryside Act of 1949. Cyril Diver was in the right place to play an active part in creating his perfect job, surrounded by friends who ensured that he was given it, and became the first Director-General of the Nature Conservancy in 1948. After retirement in 1953 he remained on the body's ruling council until 1958.

Among the pioneering designations he brought into effect on the ground were the Purbeck cluster of National Nature Reserves. Hartland Moor, half of it on the Bankes Estate, was designated in 1954, originally with permit-only access. Studland, with its original 430 acres including Little Sea and the 175-acre dune system – the second largest in the country – was established with Ralph Bankes' co-operation in 1962. The reserve was expanded across the heath, to 1,557 acres, as the landowner went through his last illness in 1981. Between them, Bankes and the Nature Conservancy had safeguarded Captain Diver's 'pet place', as first warden Bunny Teagle described it.

Studland and Arne were also adopted by Dr Norman Winfrid Moore (born 1923) who still has a holiday home on Purbeck's western coast. Oddly, on deciding he deserved a knighthood, I found he was already Sir Norman Moore, the third baronet, but declined to use the title. Norman Moore's important innovation was the concept of key indicator species, ensuring the widespread adoption of the idea as the Principal Scientific Officer of the Nature Conservancy, from 1958. By 1962 he was already observing the effects of 'climatic amelioration' though at the end of the year the weather hit back with prolonged cold of such intensity that the Dartford warbler nearly ceased to be a British breeding species.

Moore pointed out that although some two thirds of Dorset's heathland had been lost since the publication of the first Ordnance Survey map in 1811, remnants at Studland, Arne, Stoborough and the Lulworth Ranges were of a scale to remain viable, representing a definable ecosystem that could be quantified in terms of 'biomass, productivity, structure and succession'. Moore's assessment and monitoring of Studland's ecology was based on the presence and viability of indicator species. Some exist in specialised niche environments rather than occurring more widely across the heath. The population dynamics are in a state of flux as they come and go when conditions change on the ground. They remain relevant to any appraisal of the health of the heaths.

*Erica ciliaris* (Dorset heath) does much better south of Poole Harbour than in its restricted sites in Devon and Cornwall. It also survives at Morden Bog and inside Rempstone Forest, beside rides and in unplanted valley bogs, although it seems to be declining on the edge of its range. Hartland Moor is the plant's key central refuge both for the Isle of Purbeck and nationally.

*Erica tetralix* (wet heath) occurs more widely in the rest of heathland Dorset than *Erica ciliaris* which is only found in Purbeck.

Marsh gentian *(Gentiana pneumonanthe)*, with its sky-blue corolla in an inch-long tube, has to be the special flower of both Studland and Dorset. 'Very local, decreasing,' according to the *Cambridge Flora of the British Isles*, it relies on acid sphagnum bogs for its niche conditions which are often under threat, 'from Dorset and Kent, to Carmarthen, Anglesey, Yorkshire and Cumberland'.

*Corynetus arenarius*, renamed *Thiuminidium purpureum* (black dune fungus), is found in black blobs about the size of rabbit droppings, between heather clumps in the sand dunes. The change in its name inspired Nature Conservancy warden Rees Cox to produce a cartoon with one specimen proclaiming the old name name and another stating the new version. His senior regional officer coined a fungal in-joke as the caption: 'Are you pulling my hyphae?'

*Ceriagrion tenellum* (dragonfly), though common in the old claypits, particularly towards Arne and Furzebrook, is only found on the Purbeck heaths.

*Pyrrhosoma nymphula* (dragonfly) has done well at Arne in water-filled craters created by Luftwaffe bombs, dropped on a dummy decoy airfield which drew bombers away from the Royal Naval Cordite Factory on Holton Heath. It is also found in ponds and slow rivers more widely in Dorset.

*Plebeius argus* (silver-studded blue butterfly) does well in warmer pockets of heathland including regenerated areas in old gravel pits but is confined to the Purbeck and Frome valley heaths, apart from a small colony on Portland. 'They need heather for nectar and short turf nearby for basking in the sunshine on south-facing slopes that warm quickly,'

Rees Cox told me. 'Mown fire-breaks through cross-leafed heath make for excellent habitat.'

*Eumensis semele* (grayling butterfly) is found more widely on the Dorset heaths and downs.

*Lacerta agilis* (sand lizard) is confined to the Dorset heaths but can survive in reclaimed and otherwise disturbed areas provided there are banks, sand dunes or exposed edges of bomb and shell craters. The latter remain a Purbeck speciality in western parts.

*Coronella austriaca* (smooth snake) is found in areas with sand lizards, its favourite prey, but also occurs in woodland on the Bagshot bed sands and in small numbers on the other side of the Purbeck Hills.

*Lacerta vivipara* (common lizard) is still common in the Purbeck heaths and woods but less so on the hills to the south. This said, an exotic touch has come to the Channel coast with the presence of the wall lizard *(Podarcis muralis)*. Large green males are particularly conspicuous along the south-facing stone cliffs and quarries from Winspit and Seacombe to Durlston Country Park. They must be the descendants of introductions as the closest indigenous colony is between Gorey Common and Bonley Bay in the north-east corner of Jersey.

*Vipera berus berus* (adder) is a protected species which does well in much of Purbeck but experiences bad silly-season publicity out of all proportion to the risk the snake presents to human visitors, provided they wear shoes and avoid clumping through the heather.

*Sylvia undata dartfordiensis* (Dartford warbler) needs medium-sized gorse bushes, with a preference for south-facing slopes, which combine nesting spots with winter shelter and an all-year larder of insects and spiders. Having in my time been responsible for spreading the disaster story of its likely extinction, which seemed to be the situation a generation ago, I am now delighted to report that there are 120 singing males holding territories in Studland Parish in 2002. It is such a distinctive little bird, with purple breast and cocky tail, that many of us shuddered to think of our native heath without its enlivening presence. That was the case at Studland after the severe winter of 1962–63 and National Nature Reserve warden Bunny Teagle did not see one until three years after he arrived at Studland. Despite becoming a British species as a result of a specimen shot on the marshes at Dartford it has long been absent from Kent and is now regarded as the Dorset warbler.

*Saxicola torquata* (stonechat) apparently requires pine-free heathland. In this it is far fussier than the meadow pipit, the commonest heathland bird, which can survive in relatively degraded conditions. Stonechats, however, dislike what Norman Moore describes as the 'pine savannah' habitat of heather studded with self-sown trees.

The last of this checklist of significant species has been the cause of pine clearances which has joined 'rhododendron bashing' as an automatic manage-ment response to the scrubbing-up of heathland reserves. Rees Cox came to Studland from Holy Island, Lindisfarne, to take over from Bunny Teagle as the Nature Conservancy's full-time warden in 1968. He has carried out weekly butterfly and moth counts since 1976 and is also still active on the ground as a voluntary warden for the National Trust. Rees Cox cautions that the growing tendency to call in contractors to eliminate undesirable vege-tation has its pitfalls. Aspens, for instance, have fallen victim to clearances aimed at other species. There are always exceptions and even the usual targets can sometimes be of importance. In the latest case, National Trust head warden Geoff Hann inter-vened to spare a clump of condemned pines, on the South Haven peninsula. They are now the roosting trees for some 250 little egrets that breed across the water on Brownsea Island. Rees Cox explained the unusual situation:

*No one could have foreseen that two decades ago. When I reported the first little egret in 1976 my regional office sent detailed identification forms for me to complete, with a full description, so they could be sure I hadn't mistaken it for an albino heron. Now there are more little egrets breeding on Brownsea than herons.*

The numbers of long-winged conehead *(Conocephalus discolour)* suddenly exploded in the 1980s, either from genetic mutation or taking a ride on clouds of warm air from the Sahara which swept summer meadows of the Central Massif, as they crossed France. 'That was once a rarity,' said Rees Cox. 'Now it's all over the place.' At the other end of the scale, Sika deer – Dorset's largest wild animal – swam across Poole Harbour from Brownsea Island during the great fire of 1934. Others escaped from a deer park at Hyde House, between Wareham and Bere Regis, and they now number 200 or more in the area between Little Sea and Woodhouse Hill. They have munched their way through most of the royal fern for which Studland was famed in Victorian times. 'I've been putting fences around some of our best clumps,' said National Trust warden Geoff Hann. 'They particu-larly like the swamp around the lake.'

A much smaller Asiatic deer, Muntjac, descended from those which escaped from Woburn Abbey in 1940 and spread across England, are also firmly established in Purbeck. Having briefly kept four of them ('Rodney's wretched pets,' according to the author John Fowles), I am particularly adept at looking out for them, and had my first Dorset encounter below Bulbarrow, almost standing on a buck before he broke cover. Like the roe, they were always regarded as elusive, but with both species all that has now changed. In July 2002 I watched a pair of Muntjac grazing on clover in the middle of a field between Afflington Barn and Kingston, in the middle of the day, oblivious to my presence on the other side of a stone wall. There might have been another exotic species if Rees Cox had not rounded up three llamas on Studland Heath, in 1976, and returned them to Greenland Farm.

Fragmented areas of heathland soon become fragile and unstable in ecological terms, first losing key species and then eventually just about everything, except for bracken and gorse. On the other hand the vastness of Studland's heath has ensured its resilience. There have been tragedies, such as disastrous fires followed by gulls picking off surviving reptiles as they emerge from holes, but in time both fauna and flora have recovered. Restocking takes place automatically from surrounding areas. For all the concern about species reduction and endangered status I drew an almost complete blank when I asked about extinctions. It must be a mark of the success of Captain Diver's vision and his conversion of its reclusive owner, Ralph Bankes, that the Nature Conservancy not only held the line but handed over a richer tapestry of varying habitats to its successors in English Nature. Bankes also contrived a natural succession on the ground, virtually disinheriting his son, John Ralph Bankes (1937–96) – who lies in Studland churchyard – and ensuring that National Trust ownership followed. Ralph Bankes died in 1981 and left the biggest bequest in the charity's history which was conservatively valued at £25 million. Subsequent management by Geoff and Greta Hann, along with the work of Julian Homer and his other staff, has progressively balanced the pressure of 25,000 visitors a day with the preservation of the sands and wilderness they come to enjoy. Struggling to make someone name a single extinction I was eventually told, 'You could mention black game.' On checking, however, I found it has been absent from Dorset since 1900.

Hopefully extinct, according to the wardens, are terrapins which were dumped in Little Sea and might well have bred and gobbled up the palmate newts. 'One I recovered was in a bad way, its eyes half closed,' said Rees Cox. 'The water is too acidic for them. They need a lot of calcium for their shells.' He

has also encountered at least one dubious guru-like character reciting a mantra and apparently disposing of an unwanted exotic pet. This may have been a Cayman alligator.

It seems that those in the Bournemouth conurbation who bought such creatures in the booming 1990s are now finding them too expensive to keep. Others have simply outgrown their tanks. This must be the explanation for ox frogs being spotted near the Ferry Road. Tabaqui fish, close relatives of the piranha, and a snapping turtle are also on the list of suspected illegal introductions. 'Often what happens is [similar to] the Christmas dog,' said Thomas Braunbeck, who monitors similar problems for the Heidelberg Institute for Zoology in Germany. 'The animal doesn't fit in the aquarium any more, so it's thrown out.'

The problem, in and around Little Sea, arises if a pair of exotics come together in suitable conditions in the wild. *Homo sapiens*, excluding 200 pairs nesting and in a few cases breeding in Studland Parish, is also uniquely visible for study. The nudist area, extending into the dunes behind 1,000 metres of beach between Studland and Shell Bay, covers 24 acres. It came into being for what the National Trust describes as 'recreational purposes' in the 1950s and is currently marked by red-topped posts. To quote Studland Peninsula Management Plan:

*The area is identified by a prominent notice giving visitors 900 metres forewarning that naturists may be seen. The area is designated by the Trust where visitors may be naked should they wish. The site is not exclusively for naturists and may be used by all visitors in the same manner as the rest of the beach. The coast path runs directly through the naturist area.*

The Trust's policy is 'to continue to offer the present site' including provision of its own mobile cafeteria, during the summer, but 'naturism will not be permitted in any other areas'. Fires are not permitted, but happen, with barbecue parties being the usual offenders. Rees Cox's

*National Trust staff at Studland in 2002.*

*Wardens and volunteers in action for the National Trust across Studland's heath and hinterland.*

method on controlling these – 'on breasting the dunes,' as he puts it – was to establish there was no real fire risk and diplomatically ask that each fire be put out adequately when it was finished. As a result the Nature Conservancy 'Textile' – as nudists refer to a clothed person – would be rewarded with sausages:

*In first-aid training I took special note of how to deal with flesh burns, after seeing how alarmingly close those mounds of human flesh came to splattering fat and hot coals and metal.*

One day he noticed that a naturist guide, listing beaches, gave Studland five stars instead of the usual four. 'The last star tells us the warden is friendly,' he was told. 'That means you, not the National Trust.'

Past methods of controlling the colony included borrowing mounted police from the Bristol stables of the Avon and Somerset Constabulary. It was popular with the force, as healthy exercise at the seaside for officers and mounts, but caused environmental havoc. Cavalry-style charges did more damage than the naturists. Law enforcement then became covert with surveillance followed by court cases, some involving 'undercover officers' and prison sentences, to give Studland more unwanted headlines. There was even an anti-naturist resolution at a National Trust annual general meeting but this was thrown out when no one turned up to propose it.

Rising sea levels, increased coastal erosion, and a 'managed retreat' response to seaside dynamics are arousing controversy. The National Trust finds itself pressured to preserve and protect beach huts in a

futile gesture that might as well include Julian Homer sitting in a chair between the tide-lines as a latter-day King Canute. The huts have already been moved back towards Dragon's Teeth anti-invasion defences, which stand a better chance of surviving the new century. Even Fort Henry, on Redend Point, is being undermined.

Part of the problem is that the large-scale accretion of sand between Shell Bay and Studland, which continued into the late-twentieth century, had its origins elsewhere in Poole Bay. Victorian iron-stone workings caused Hengistbury Head to shrink inland from the Beerpan Rocks and led to the hotels dropping down the cliffs of Southbourne. They were still doing that in the 1950s. That source of sand supply, which took decades to work its way westwards, has been stopped by promenades and groynes. The result of stabilisation of the Bournemouth coastline is that currents around Studland no longer deposit fresh sand.

'Parking spaces at Knoll Beach are fast being lost to the sea,' the Trust reports, although so far the losses have taken place when they are empty. Bournemouth University students found that forecast losses for a 25-year period were being lost in a single year. A total of 190 car spaces at Knoll Beach had to be abandoned in 1998 alone:

*On a busy day there may be 3,000 cars parked on the peninsula. Given the speed of erosion and time scale necessary to develop an alternative transport system, planning permission will be sought to build a false dune along the Knoll car park to act as a temporary sea defence and provide time for managed retreat.*

Above: *Building a bird-hide in the National Trust workshop at Studland.*

Below: *Landscaping Middle Beach car park.*

# Conservation

*Drainage work and a bird-hide in place, plus a nesting box for barn owls (actually used by a pair of kestrels).*

# Conservation

*Geoff Hann (left) and wardens at work.*

*The main reason for erosion appears to be climate change. There has been an increase in easterly winds, and stormy weather generally, as well as a rise in sea level. South Beach and Middle Beach are now very narrow especially at low tide. Increasing amounts of seaweed have been washed ashore, which in many Trust properties would cause no problem, but at Studland arouses a considerable number of complaints. Though a natural part of the shoreline ecology, much of it has been cleared, to minimise smell and reduce the visual effect.*

Seaweed does not fit with the public perception of Studland beach. Most visitors are attracted by golden sands and the safest of British beaches. In the opinion of many of us it is the best in the country. Others come to bird-watch, particularly out of season when 3,000 duck and geese descend on Little Sea, but even in summertime only one per cent of visitors venture far into the surrounding heath. On the other hand, seawards to Swanage, the chalky track beside Old Harry Rocks is one of the busiest lengths of the 650-mile South West Coast Path which starts at Shell Bay. Beyond Dorset and Devon it goes round the Lizard and Land's End to Minehead in Somerset.

Although an estimated 20,000 to 25,000 people succeed in reaching Studland on warmer days in high summer and over holiday weekends, a similar number abandon the attempt when they encounter chronic congestion. Police are sometimes forced to close the road at Corfe Castle. The longer-term solution to access would be a park-and-ride system to decant visitors into land-trams at Norden and carry them along the line of the former Goathorn Railway. Collaboration with the Ryder Estate, to enable the crossing of Rempstone Forest, would be necessary. The idea is being mooted as a practical way to relieve pressure on the ferry in the north and reduce traffic through the village in the south.

Both in Studland village and at Shell Bay the National Trust owns most of the land. Although it has sold some choice homes – prices of around £225,000 were breathtaking at the time but have since been eclipsed by valuations of over £1,000,000 – the Trust still owns many houses and other properties. The full list includes Fort Henry, three toilet blocks, the village cart shed, and 260 beach huts. Groom's Cottage has become the 'Police Community' contact point and interview room. Of the more substantial occupied buildings, half are used by the Trust in its operations or as staff accommodation, and the others are leased.

Regular events in village life include Studland Country Fair, across a long weekend each August, and the Bankes Arms Beer Festival. There is also a Bankes Arms Irish Festival. 'Z' is for zoning in the National Trust lexicon and as such in Studland there are times and areas set aside for a whole raft of leisure activities. Not all are compatible on the same stretch of land or water and there is a policy for dealing with this:

## NT & Other Businesses

Bankes Arms Hotel
Estate Workshop, Middle Beach
Isle of Purbeck Golf Club
Knoll Cafe, Knoll Beach
Middle Beach Café and Shop
Shell Bay Café and Chandlery
Studland Stores

Countryside Office, Middle Beach
Groom's Cottage and Stable Block, Middle Beach
Joe's Cafe, South Beach
Manor House Hotel
Old Coastguard Buildings
Shell Bay Restaurant and Boathouse
Study Base, Knoll Beach

## Farms

Greenland Farm          Harmony Farm          Manor Farm

## Houses

Agglestone Cottage
Cliff End
Groom's Cottage
Leaze Cottages (Numbers 1 and 2)
Marine Terrace (Numbers 1 to 5)
School Lane (Number 11)
Wadmore Farmhouse
Woodhouse (Numbers 44 and 45)

Alma Terrace (Number 4)
Dairy House
Harry Warren House
Manor Cottage
Old School House
Smugglers Watch
Watery Lane (Numbers 2 and 3)

Beach Cottage
The Green (Number 24)
Langtoft
Manor Farm Cottage
Pippin Cottage
Wadmore Cottage
Wood End

# PC Plod

Enid Blyton's character, based on Studland
village policeman Christopher Rone, returns
with Inspector Nick Mason to open the new
Police Post in Groom's Cottage, photographed
by Samantha Cook in July 2002.

> ### BEACH PURSUITS
> BAIT DIGGING *(in Bramble Bush Bay)*
> BARBECUES *(restricted to designated areas)*
> BEACH HUTS *(which have a five-year waiting list)*
> BIRD-WATCHING *(from hides at Little Sea and Bramble Bush Bay)*
> BOATING *(up to 300 vessels on a busy weekend in Studland Bay)*
> CAMPING *(being discouraged)*
> CYCLING *(the Trust welcomes cyclists on its land)*
> DISABLED ACCESS *(short wheelchair routes into sand dunes, heath and woods)*
> DOG WALKING *(summertime restrictions on the beaches)*
> EDUCATIONAL VISITS *(all year round)*
> FIELD STUDIES *(ecology, geology and geomorphology)*
> GOLFING *(Isle of Purbeck Golf Club)*
> HORSE RIDING *(bridleways or by permit)*
> HOUSEBOATS *(five in Bramble Bush Bay)*
> JET SKIS *(prohibited from launching or landing)*
> METAL DETECTING *(only on the beach)*
> MOUNTAIN BIKING *(legal on bridleways)*
> NATURAL HISTORY STUDIES *(mainly on the heath)*
> NATURISM *(designated area between Studland and Shell Bay)*
> PARKING *(being restricted to the main car parks)*
> SAILING *(from a small boat park next to Knoll Beach slipway)*
> SUNBATHING *(on and beside the main beaches)*
> SWIMMING *(at Studland)*
> TREASURE HUNTING *(metal detectors allowed only on the beaches)*
> WALKING *(on the coast path and across the heath and hills)*
> WIND SURFING *(although conditions are usually too calm)*

*Where possible any conflicts between user groups should be resolved by identifying the nature of the conflict and adopting appropriate management in conjunction with the users themselves.*

Wardening on the beaches and nature reserves currently caters for – or controls – a variety of uses and pursuits. Most have been provided with their own explanatory leaflets *(see panel above)*.

One conflict has never stirred emotions on the Studland peninsula. Hunting, game-shooting and wildfowling have not taken place in the eastern harbour and heath in living memory, though Richard Ryder is remembered for seeing off otter hunters from Rempstone at the end of a shotgun in the 1960s. Traditionally, both for the Bankes Estate and its National Trust successors, most of the income needed for the maintenance of their land in the Isle of Purbeck has come from Studland beach. It is a satisfying thought that landscape can be financially self-sustaining and the polluter made to pay for the upkeep of one of the most beautiful but fragile pieces of British scenery. No wonder Studland is such a desirable place.

The ultimate irony of the best run National Trust property in the land is that it so nearly never happened. The obvious 'what if' is that had Ralph Bankes behaved like a normal person he would never have given his entire estate to the nation. For Studland, however, the miracle happened not once in the twentieth century but twice over. It came as a revelation to me – although I

was well aware of threats from cable-car tramways – but this had far greater implications. The best of my finds did not come to light until the final note-taking session during my research for this book at Studland Countryside Office in September 2002. I was being told by countryside manager Julian Homer how dairying and its slurry problems had ended. Harmony Farm been allowed to revert to nature and was now walking country, grazed by Exmoor ponies between Studland and Purbeck Golf Club, and we were discussing ways of encouraging villagers to make more use of their newly-provided leisure land. A similar network of paths through the trees on Woodhouse Hill also has signs but remains a well-kept secret. 'Even the dog walkers don't go there,' Julian sighed.

In walked the ex-village Bobby, sometime beach inspector for the Bankes Estate, and since 1982 the National Trust chief warden. Geoff Hann was holding a heavy framed poster offering Studland for sale as building plots. It dated from after the death of Walter Bankes, when son Ralph was a child, and the estate trustees needed to raise money after the Armistice in 1918. The steward, Major Alfred Thomas Lodder, instructed Wimborne land agents Henry Richards and Son to prepare the sale prospectus for 'Studland Bay Freehold Building Estate'. This advanced as far as typesetting for printing but then something happened to cause a change of mind. On advice from the auctioneers the village of Holt was sold instead. That was Studland's miraculous escape.

# Studland's Lucky Escape

*National Trust property manager Julian Homer offering 'Studland Bay Freehold Building Estate'
in a poster for a sale that was cancelled.*

# SUBSCRIBERS

Lucy and David Annat

The Apsey family, Corfe Castle, Dorset

J. Peter Arnold, Great Hale, Lincolnshire

John A. Barnes CBE, Poole, Dorset

Major and Mrs N. Bate, Studland, Dorset

A.C. Baxter, Little Woolgarston, Corfe Castle, Dorset

Peggy Bessant, Wareham, Dorset

Richard, Mandy, Emma-Jay, Charlotte and Matthew Best, Studland, Dorset

Trevor Betts, Beaminster, Dorset

Erik and Janet Bjorkstrand

Charles A.F. Blair, Canford Cliffs, Dorset

Pamela Blandford, Studland, Dorset

Julia M. Blaxill, Bournemouth, Dorset

Garry E. Bower, Sandford, Nr Wareham, Dorset

Peter Bowyer, Studland, Dorset

Andrew D. Bracey, Ruislip, Middlesex

Victor Brindley, Swanage, Dorset

Don G. Bromby, Falmouth, Cornwall

Mr S.G. Brooks, Bovington, Dorset

Heather Broomfield, Studland, Dorset

Aurthur and Janet Brown, Hoburne Park, Swanage, Dorset

Philip and Joan Bruton

Michael Burge and Emma Parker-Drake, Swanage, Dorset

Norman J. Burrell, Wareham, Dorset

Merle and Bob Chacksfield, Swanage, Dorset

Joyce N. Chant (née Battrick), Wareham, Dorset

Mrs Brenda Charles, Sandbanks, Dorset

M.J. Cheesman, Studland, Dorset

Doris E. Churchill, Studland, Dorset

Ian C. Sutton Clark, Wareham, Dorset

Margaret Clark, Studland, Dorset

Richard Clarkson, St Paul's Cray, Kent

Barbara Clayton, Studland, Dorset

John T. Connor, Studland, Dorset

Joan and John Cook

Judith Coulter, Holmfirth, West Yorkshire

Rees Cox, English Nature Warden, Studland Heath NNR 1968–96

George Crane, Swanage, Dorset

Joanna Crichton, Wareham, Dorset

The Family Cripps, Poole, Dorset

Michael and Dawn Cuthbertson, Canford Cliffs, Dorset

Keith and Margaret Dando, Studland, Dorset

Kirsty De'Ath, Studland, Dorset

Roger Deakin, The Glebe, Studland, Dorset

Barbara and Clem Dennis, Swanage, Dorset

Carol Dexter, Bricket Wood, Hertfordshire

Michael Dexter, Radlett, Hertfordshire

Diane Doyle, Chicago, USA

Mr W.G. Dye, Swanage, Dorset

Simon J. Ellis, Southampton

The Ferguson Family, Studland, Dorset

Susan Fielder, Bristol

Christopher G. Finch, Redbourn, Hertfordshire

Fran and Mike Frith, Swanage, Dorset

Colin and Sylvia Garrett, Swanage, Dorset

Michael Gater B.Sc., FRICS, Northampton

Captain Alex W.R. Gibbons, Swanage, Dorset

Philip Goldenberg, Studland, Dorset

Brigadier H. John Goodson OBE, Poole, Dorset

Mrs Monica Gracey (née Clark), formerly of Studland

David and Molly (née Clark) Grant, formerly of Studland, Dorset

David and Sheila Griffiths, Sandbanks

Jan and Roy Gwilliam, Swanage, Dorset

Tim and Clare Haggett, Arne and Western Australia

Iris Haighton, Studland, Dorset

Peter Hammond

Andrew Hawkes, Poole, Dorset

Julie Hazlett, Waterlooville, Hants.

Jane and Simon Henty, Burford, Oxfordshire

Arthur and Barbara Hepher, N. Chailey, Sussex

Mrs Pat Heron (formerly Wheeler), Wareham, Dorset

Anthony and Felicity Higgins, The Old School House, Studland, Dorset

Joy F.A. Hill (née Summers), Corfe Castle, Dorset

Mrs Jean Hodgson, Sandbanks, Dorset

Daphne E. Howell, Canford Cliffs, Poole, Dorset

Mrs E. Hunt, Swanage, Dorset

Major John Ives, Studland, Dorset

Linda M. Jackson (née Battrick), Studland, Dorset

Mr and Mrs P.F. Janes, Studland, Dorset

Mrs S.A. Jeans, Parkstone, Poole, Dorset

Bob Jones, Bury St Edmunds, Suffolk

Anne and Michael King, Wareham, Dorset

Teresa Lawton, Studland, Dorset

Mrs G. Lee, The Glebe, Studland, Dorset

Leeson House Field Studies Centre

Damond J. Lock, Studland, Dorset

Bill Marshallsay (deceased)

John J. Matthews, Bournemouth, Dorset

Ian Methven

Jack and June Morrell, Swanage, Dorset

David and Barbara Murray

Miss J. Murrey, Ewell, Surrey

Dr and Mrs Martin Neary, Studland, Dorset

Ruth Norton, Corfe Castle, Dorset

P.C. Peter Norton, Studland, Dorset 1978–2000

Dennis Oakes, Poole, Dorset

Michael and Valerie Oxley, Poole, Dorset

Bruce and Joy Peppin, Kenton, Middlesex

Christopher and Megan Peppin, Oxhey, Hertfordshire

David and Zoe Peppin, Chorleywood, Hertfordshire

Steve and Fridolin Peppin, Harrow on the Hill, Middlesex

Margaret Perkins, Swanage, Dorset

Peter and Wendy Phillips, Studland, Dorset

Mr G.R. Porter, Swanage, Dorset

Edward and Jo Pratt, Swanage, Dorset

Gary and Karen Prescott, Swanage, Dorset

Stephen Ranger, Swanage, Dorset

Pammie Rayment, Studland, Dorset

Nichola Reavenall, New Cross, London

Alastair Richardson, Sansted Mountfitchet, Essex

Carol Richardson, Swanage, Dorset

Ruth and Russell Riddy, Studland, Dorset

Richard T. Riding

Frank Roberts, Swanage, Dorset

Richard N. Rose, Studland, Dorset

Simon P. Rowbrey, Sandbanks, Dorset

Ken and Phyl Saunders, Swanage, Dorset

Rev. Frank Scammell, Former Vicar of Studland

Derek Sharp, Wareham, Dorset

Del Shilton, Coventry

Richard Slowe

Sydney E. Smith

Col and Mrs D.J. Squirrell

Eric St. C. Stobart, Studland, Dorset

D. Stratton, Studland, Dorset

F. Stratton, Studland, Dorset

Studland Women's Institute

Violet Styles, Studland, Dorset

Martin Summers

Bill and Anne Summers

Neil Sutherland, Studland, Dorset

Vanessa Sutherland, Studland, Dorset

Arthur and Ann Tait, Arne

Stephen Tansey, Canford Cliffs, Dorset

Graham D. Tarrant, Stoborough, Dorset

Grace Taylor, Studland, Dorset

R. Thompson family

Keith and Monica Twining-Smith, Branksome Park, Poole, Dorset

Simon Vincent Vautier-Wilson, Dorset

June Walker, Swanage, Dorset

John F.W. Walling, Newton Abbot, Devon

Jim and Barbara Walsh, Northampton

Michael H. Walshaw, Swanage, Dorset

Nicholas Warner, Goathorn, Studland, Dorset

Angela K. Waterman, Studland, Dorset

Nigel Watts FCA, Sandbanks, Poole, Dorset

John G. Way, Wool, Dorset

Max and Sharon Welby, The Glebe, Studland, Dorset

Terence G. and Valerie L. West, Worth Matravers, Dorset

Matthew Western, Berkswell, West Warwickshire

Raymond C. Western, Corfe Castle, Dorset

Mary E.G. Wharton, Swanage, Dorset

Dave and Sue Whitton, Swanage, Dorset

David and Fran Witherby, Studland, Dorset

Marion K. Wood, Stoborough, Dorset

Pauline and Bruce Wood, East Swanage, Dorset

Thomas Yeatman, Swanage, Dorset

# FURTHER TITLES

## *Titles from the Series*

*The Book of Addiscombe* • Various
*The Book of Addiscombe, Vol. II* • Various
*The Book of Bampton* • Caroline Seward
*The Book of Barnstaple* • Avril Stone
*Book of Bickington* • Stuart Hands
*Blandford Forum: A Millennium Portrait* • Various
*The Book of Bridestowe* • R. Cann
*The Book of Brixham* • Frank Pearce
*The Book of Buckland Monachorum & Yelverton* • Hemery
*The Book of Carshalton* • Stella Wilks
*The Parish Book of Cerne Abbas* • Vale & Vale
*The Book of Chagford* • Ian Rice
*The Book of Chittlehamholt with*
*Warkleigh & Satterleigh* • Richard Lethbridge
*The Book of Chittlehampton* • Various
*The Book of Colney Heath* • Bryan Lilley
*The Book of Constantine* • Moore & Trethowan
*The Book of Cornwood & Lutton* • Various
*The Book of Creech St Michael* • June Small
*The Book of Cullompton* • Various
*The Book of Dawlish* • Frank Pearce
*The Book of Dulverton, Brushford,*
*Bury & Exebridge* • Various
*The Book of Dunster* • Hilary Binding
*The Ellacombe Book* • Sydney R. Langmead
*The Book of Exmouth* • W.H. Pascoe
*The Book of Grampound with Creed* • Bane & Oliver
*The Book of Hayling Island & Langstone* • Rogers
*The Book of Helston* • Jenkin with Carter
*The Book of Hemyock* • Clist & Dracott
*The Book of Hethersett* • Various
*The Book of High Bickington* • Avril Stone
*The Book of Ilsington* • Dick Wills
*The Book of Lamerton* • Ann Cole & Friends
*Lanner, A Cornish Mining Parish* • Scharron Schwartz & Roger Parker
*The Book of Leigh & Bransford* • Various
*The Book of Litcham with Lexham & Mileham* • Various
*The Book of Loddiswell* • Various
*The Book of Lulworth* • Rodney Legg
*The Book of Lustleigh* • Joe Crowdy
*The Book of Manaton* • Various
*The Book of Markyate* • Various
*The Book of Mawnan* • Various
*The Book of Meavy* • Pauline Hemery
*The Book of Minehead with Alcombe* • Binding & Stevens
*The Book of Morchard Bishop* • Jeff Kingaby
*The Book of Newdigate* • John Callcut
*The Book of Northlew with Ashbury* • Various
*The Book of North Newton* • Robins & Robins
*The Book of North Tawton* • Various
*The Book of Okehampton* • Radford & Radford
*The Book of Paignton* • Frank Pearce
*The Book of Penge, Anerley & Crystal Palace* • Various
*The Book of Peter Tavy with Cudlipptown* • Various
*The Book of Pimperne* • Jean Coull
*The Book of Plymtree* • Tony Eames
*The Book of Porlock* • Denis Corner
*Postbridge – The Heart of Dartmoor* • Reg Bellamy
*The Book of Priddy* • Various
*The Book of Rattery* • Various
*The Book of Silverton* • Various
*The Book of South Molton* • Various

## *Titles from the Series continued*

*The Book of South Stoke* • Various
*South Tawton & South Zeal with Sticklepath* • Radfords
*The Book of Sparkwell with Hemerdon & Lee Mill* • Pam James
*The Book of Staverton* • Pete Lavis
*The Book of Stithians* • Various
*The Book of Studland* • Rodney Legg
*The Book of Swanage* • Rodney Legg
*The Book of Torbay* • Frank Pearce
*Uncle Tom Cobley & All: Widecombe-in-the-Moor* • Stephen Woods
*The Book of Watchet* • Compiled by David Banks
*The Book of West Huntspill* • Various
*Widecombe-in-the-Moor* • Stephen Woods
*The Book of Williton* • Michael Williams
*Woodbury: The Twentieth Century Revisited* • Roger Stokes
*The Book of Woolmer Green* • Various

## *Forthcoming*

*The Book of Bakewell* • Various
*The Book of Barnstaple, Vol. II* • Avril Stone
*The Book of Brampford* • Various
*The Book of Breage & Gurmoe* • Stephen Polglase
*The Book of the Bedwyns* • Various
*The Book of Bideford* • Peter Christie
*The Book of Bridport* • Rodney Legg
*The Book of Buckfastleigh* • Sandra Coleman
*The Book of Carharrack* • Various
*The Book of Castleton* • Geoff Hill
*The Book of Edale* • Gordon Miller
*The Book of Kingskerswell* • Various
*The Book of Lostwithiel* • Barbara Frasier
*The Book of Lydford* • Barbara Weeks
*The Book of Lyme Regis* • Rodney Legg
*The Book of Nether Stowey* • Various
*The Book of Nynehead* • Various
*The Book of Princetown* • Dr Gardner-Thorpe
*The Book of St Day* • Various
*The Book of Sampford Courtenay
with Honeychurch* • Stephanie Pouya
*The Book of Sculthorpe* • Garry Windeler
*The Book of Sherborne* • Rodney Legg
*The Book of Southbourne* • Rodney Legg
*The Book of Tavistock* • Gerry Woodcock
*The Book of Thorley* • Various
*The Book of Tiverton* • Mike Sampson
*The Book of West Lavington* • Various
*The Book of Witheridge* • Various
*The Book of Withycombe* • Chris Boyles

For details of any of the above titles or if you are
interested in writing your own history, please contact: Commissioning Editor Community Histories, Halsgrove House,
Lower Moor Way, Tiverton Business Park, Tiverton, Devon EX16 6SS, England;
email: naomic@halsgrove.com

In order to include as many historic photographs as
possible in this volume, a printed index is not included.
However, the Community History Series is indexed by
Genuki. For further information and indexes to
volumes in the series, please visit:
http://www.cs.ncl.uk/genuki/DEV/indexingproject.html